T0028241

*The Lost Colony
of the Confederacy*

MILITARY HISTORY SERIES ☆ TEXAS A&M UNIVERSITY ☆
69

The Lost Colony of the Confederacy

EUGENE C. HARTER

TEXAS A&M UNIVERSITY PRESS
College Station

Library of Congress Cataloging-in-Publication Data

Harter, Eugene C.
    The lost colony of the Confederacy / Eugene C. Harter.
    p. cm.
    Originally published: University Press of Mississippi, 1985.
    Includes index.
    ISBN 1-58544-102-3
    1. Americans—Brazil—History—19th century. 2. American
Confederate voluntary exiles—Brazil—History—19th century.
3. United States—History—Civil War, 1861–1865—Refugees.
4. Americana (Brazil)—History. I. Title.

F2659.A5 H37 2000
 981.004'13—dc21   00-037803

For Dorothy

Contents

Preface

One of the most imposing and least-known monuments in the United States is located in Todd County, Kentucky, at the birthplace of Jefferson Davis, president of the Confederate States of America. It is a massive obelisk, 350 feet high, a somewhat smaller version of the Washington monument in the District of Columbia. When I visited the site in 1962, few others were visiting it, and the memorial was beginning to crumble. The elevator to the top was out of commission; there were cracks in the concrete; dust was everywhere.

Five thousand miles away, in southern Brazil, there exists another Confederate monument, much like the one in Kentucky, though smaller. This obelisk, its sides well scrubbed, stands among the graves of Confederate voluntary exiles, their relatives, and descendants.

This book is about the grim, quixotic journey of twenty thousand or so Confederates to Brazil at the end of the American Civil War. In that faraway country, the Confederados, as they were known to the Brazilians, found a way to continue their way of life, free of contact with the military conqueror. It was a solution to the dilemma of living in a changed South, where defeat and invasion by the Yankees threatened that tender essence of community and customs that defined the southerner. In Brazil southerners could survive with honor.

The cultural province they established still exists, testifying to the hardiness of American ways. Perhaps one of the best ways to get a good view of their descendants is to attend one of the Fourth of July picnics in the park near the church at the Confederate Cemetery, near the city of Americana. The picnic could be an anthropologist's treasure trove. Two distinctive societies, Brazilian and American, have blended into each other. The Confederate descendants, bilingual and with a definite Scotch-Irish look about them, get more than just a second glance from camera-laden, brightly clad American tourists. The experience is something like staring into a mirror and seeing your own image, slightly askew. Could it be the look in the eye, the body language, the darker skin? Before you are southern descendants who have not experienced the last one hundred thirty years of North-South, black-white cleavage familiar to their cousins in the U.S.A.

Oddly, in looking over the vast record of the Civil War and the Reconstruction era the researcher will not find a book published in the United States about the migration of Confederates to Brazil, though the exodus was a household word at the time and an indicator of the blue-hot resentment against the northern invaders and the strict measures imposed by the federal government after the peace of Appomattox. Unless the record of postwar emigration is added to the mix of history, the story will remain incomplete, a gilded picture of events in the South then and now and another triumph of "public relations" over truth. This silence has also played a part in distorting the record of these stateless last Confederates, who once again challenged the frontiers, were culturally Latinized over time, and became "os Confederados."

I am content in this book just to seed this little-plowed ground, to introduce the subject of this lost colony to the reader. It is a portion of a larger story, a sampling rather than an inventory. I do not mean it to be a travelogue. In this and other writings on the subject I have occasionally drawn from oral history—having the good luck to have the participants in the story across from me at the family dinner table—and from boyhood memories of my mother sitting in the parlor of our home on the beach in Ipanema, Brazil, playing "Dixie" on the upright piano. I was born in Rio de Janeiro, Brazil, and was raised in the Confederate colony there. My grandparents and great grandparents, from Mississippi and Texas, were members of this southward caravan. They survived the perilous journey to carve a life for themselves and their children among the Brazilians.

Unlike most of the Confederados, I returned (*returned* is not exactly the word, but somehow it seems proper) to America in 1935, together with my mother, father, brother, and sister. We lived for a while in Meridian, Mississippi, then moved to Ohio where Father found work as a newspaper reporter and insurance salesman, counting himself lucky to obtain employment in the midst of America's worst economic depression.

In America we began to realize that we were (and still are) a unique blend—part Brazilian, part Confederate, and now American. We realized that we were, to some degree, the last Confederates, preserved in the amber of a South American society. We had not experienced the same kind of trauma and change that had overtaken the southerners who stayed in the United States after the Civil War and Reconstruction period, and we had to learn about the unique race relations, the bizarre breakfast foods like Rice Krispies, the mating habits, the sports (U.S. football was a game played with a ball that had points on it), and how different northerners and southerners were from each other.

It was not until thirty-six years after my arrival that I returned to Brazil. After graduation from Wittenberg University in Ohio and fourteen years as a journalist on midwestern and southern newspapers, I joined the United States Foreign Service. Diplomatic appointments in Beirut, Lebanon, and Mexico City preceded my assignment as United States consul in Brazil in 1971.

It was a marvelous adventure of rediscovery. Old friends and relatives welcomed me back into the Brazilian society. I traveled about the country visiting many of the Confederate descendants, noting how they had become assimilated into the Brazilian cultural landscape, yet had retained a measure of American ways. At the Confederate cemetery near Americana (the city of 160,000 inhabitants founded by the migrant Confederates), I visited the grave of my grandmother and picnicked with fellow descendants nearby in the midst of palms, Alabama pine trees, and bougainvillea. Many times, speaking both in English and Portuguese, we conversed long into the night about the cross-cultural lives we were leading. The Confederados had many questions about the United States and were surprised to learn that very few Americans, even southerners, had ever heard of their forefathers' exodus to Brazil.

As a consequence, I made it a point to invite visiting Americans, especially journalists, to the Confederate grounds, hoping that they would take the word back home. Some, including Warren Hoge of the *New York Times*, Edgar Miller of the Associated Press, and Steve Yolen of UPI, did write excellent essays about these last Confederates. When the governor of Georgia visited Brazil in 1972 it seemed appropriate to show him the southern legacy these transplanted Americans had preserved. A crowd of about two hundred descendants gathered at the cemetery in Americana, where the flags of Brazil, the United States, and the Confederacy hung side by side, to meet the American governor and hear him speak.

Jimmy (how southern that name seemed to us) Carter, Rosalynn, and press assistant Jodie Powell were surprised that such a colony existed. When Carter came face to face with the descendants, tears rolled down his cheeks and he turned away for an instant. I walked him past the tombstones. One, near the palms at the entrance, was inscribed, "Private Jonathan Ellsworth, drummer boy of the First Arkansas Brigade." Some of the tombstones were engraved in English; others in Portuguese; some in both languages.

On returning home, in an interview published in the *Atlanta Constitution* on June 11, 1972, Carter described his emotions.

> My primary feeling was one of appreciation for their preserving in an almost unblemished way in names, inflections and voices of their ancestors their obvious love for the United States. My most significant feeling was one of great sadness they had foregone for all those generations the enjoyment of being a part of this nation they still revere so deeply. The futility of it all was apparent. None of them looked upon their ancestors as mistaken. They didn't seem to feel any self-pity.

Carter supposed there might be similarities between the exiled Southerners' feelings for their former country and the feelings of the Jewish people for Israel. "The most remarkable thing was," said Carter, "when they spoke they sounded just like people in south Georgia."

Other visitors, too, have noted the "Americanness" of these last Confederates in Brazil. It is evident not only in their language but in their customs and attitudes. Rather than mere curiosities of history, the last Confederates offer a view of America's past and, perhaps, uncover a piece of our cultural puzzle.

The effects of the American Civil War and, more, the sectional differences that caused it are with us yet, though the late nineteenth-century influx of immigrants from Europe to the U.S. has diverted the North's attention and obscured America's differences. But the South's attention is less diverted. Not long ago, a friend of mine from Raeford, South Carolina, said to me, "It would be better if people would just stop talking about the war." The grim conviction with which he uttered the words makes the incident easy to recall. What he meant was that it made him mad every time he thought of it. But the bloody American Civil War is a recent event by most historical standards. Through the years, America's recollection of the struggle seems to dim a bit, but a certain uneasiness remains, though it is not fashionable to dwell on it. The fires have cooled, but it is useful to understand how intense were the feelings that sparked the migration to Brazil and other areas of the globe. Because of the Confederate migration, Brazil too has felt the effects of the U.S. war. Southern ways have melded into Brazilian in that other great melting pot, and none of us can ever go back. We are linked by the unbreakable bonds of history.

Acknowledgments

First, I offer my appreciation to my wife, Dorothy, whose love, dedication, and wisdom motivated the project to its completion.

Also I thank my friends and cousins, the Confederados of Brazil, for the stories recounted over many cups of cafezinho.

My appreciation, too, goes to Brazilian historian Judith Jones, whose *Soldado Descansa* (*Soldier, Now You May Rest!*) has kept the memory alive. Many others have supplied material and insights through conversations and correspondence. I am grateful to James Jones, James Carr, Alice Ferro, Thelma Huber, Pamela Huber, Charles Freligh, John Logue, Ruy Barbosa, Charles McFadden, Christiano Whitaker, and Betty Thomas Antunes de Oliveira. The Latin American Division of the Library of Congress, the Georgia Department of Archives, the Washington College Library, the Kent County Library in Chestertown, Maryland, my children Gene, Ann, David, and Melissa, editor Seetha Srinivasan, and literary agent, Ann Buchwald were all helpful to this work. My special thanks go to my sister, Lucia Gooding, who also lived the story, and to Mississippi ETV producer Edward Cohen, who invited me to participate in his *The Last Confederates*, a 1984 PBS television documentary that deserves a place in the U.S. national historical record, and should be viewed by all Americans.

Our thanks to the country of Brazil, a nation of generous people who provided sanctuary for my grandparents and their fellow colonists.

Finally, to Mãe and Pop, who encountered the effects of two migrations, and overcame them.

THE LOST COLONY
OF THE CONFEDERACY

ATLANTIC OCEAN

AMAZON RIVER

Santarem

BRAZIL

Rio Doce

Americana

Campinas

São Paulo

Rio de Janeiro

Juquiá
New Texas
Xiririca

Scale of Miles

0————————500

ATLANTIC OCEAN

Principal Confederate Settlements in Brazil

ONE

The Eternal Remembrance

I N the United States, there had been several movements to abolish slavery gradually. None of them caught on. Newspaper editor Elijah P. Lovejoy in 1833 proposed using the system the British had employed in the West Indies to solve the American problem. The British Parliament had voted twenty thousand pounds sterling—approximately seventy million dollars or four hundred dollars per slave—to reimburse the planters for the loss of property. An apprentice system was also set up for the freed slaves.[1]

To have paid at that rate for the three million slaves in the United States would have cost over a billion dollars, a monstrous figure at the time. Nor would slaveholders have agreed to this payment, for it was far less than the going price for a slave in the U.S. Northern taxpayers, at the same time, refused to allow such a large outpouring of public funds. Yet the Civil War cost 600,000 lives, more than six billion dollars in taxes, and uncalculated destruction of property.

Lincoln, even after emancipation, clung to the idea of reimbursing southerners, to some degree at least, for their lost property. As late as February 1864 he held that the North and South were both responsible for slavery, and he proposed to his cabinet a $400 million appropriation for reimbursement, provided that the Confederates ceased hostilities by April 1 of that year. The cabinet unanimously opposed the idea.[2] Lincoln laid it aside, temporarily, he thought, but his assassination put an end to the notion of reimbursing a defeated South.

Pre–Civil War America, North and South, was walking a

3

tightrope by permitting the morally unsupportable system of slavery. In the northern mind the plantation slaveholder was, to some degree, a prisoner of his own economic system. Although many in the North repudiated the system of plantation slavery, they were reluctant to act precipitously to abolish it. Northerners, too, had owned slaves in colonial America, and they had profited from the slave trade and from the cotton produced by slave labor. Even in antebellum times, many northerners realized that they shared the blame with southerners for the existence of the peculiar institution.

The United States maintained its unity in the turbulent 1830s, 1840s, and 1850s through the sheer determination of its leaders and citizenry to muddle through to a solution of the problem. The Abolition movement grew through these decades, becoming a sort of catalyst for division. In the end, the organized Abolitionists, considered radical even in the North, attacked southern slaveholders without restraint, piling vituperation and invective on the heads of southerners and stinging their pride. Conflicts between North and South over tariff questions and the expansion of slavery to the western territories kept the pot boiling and increasingly alienated the South.

In a national spirit of wishful thinking, America postponed the inevitable, seeking to avoid a cataclysmic, possibly suicidal war more horrifying than the institution of slavery. Men like Daniel Webster of Massachusetts and John C. Calhoun of South Carolina fashioned one compromise after another, using all their oratorical talents to hold the country together.

At last, compromise was no longer possible. Their resentment overflowing, the southern states seceded from the Union. President Lincoln ordered the army to oppose the withdrawal by force of arms. The new Confederacy determined to resist the armed invasion of its territory. And thus, in the 1860s Americans finally got around to killing each other.

GESTURE OF DEFIANCE

My grandfather, John Wesley Harris, and his brother, William, were youngsters living near Meridian, Mississippi, in February

1864, when General William Tecumseh Sherman came through on his Meridian Campaign. The two boys watched the Union army plunder and burn the little town. "It was something," Grandfather recalled many years later, "that the North could take little pride from, not the kind of stuff likely to occupy the memorial plaques on the walls of West Point Military Academy. It was not a military maneuver with plumed hats, bugles sounding and troops on parade. Just scattered Union troops, stealing and burning everything—forcing starvation on the women and children."

Though only a small settlement of about a hundred persons at the beginning of the war, Meridian had importance far beyond its size. It was the crossroads of two important railroads, the Mobile & Ohio and the Vicksburg & Montgomery. Thus, it was an ideal location for the Confederate military headquarters. Meridian quickly became a wartime boomtown, crammed with troops, suppliers, and camp followers. Considered safe from Union attack, the town became the repository of the Mississippi state records in 1863. But the following year General Sherman's marauding troops made their appearance.

The ambitious Sherman, in his official report, wrote: "For five days, 10,000 men worked hard with a will in that work of destruction with axes, crowbars, sledges, clawbars and fire, and I have no hesitation in pronouncing the work well done. Meridian, with its depots, storehouses, arsenal, hospitals, offices, hotels and cantonments, no longer exists."[3] It was the first exhibition of Sherman's considerable skill in the art of warring on the civilian population by destroying everything in the path of his advancing forces. Jefferson Davis referred to the general's army as "worse than vandal hordes." Shelby Foote eloquently described the desolation Sherman's "bummers," as they were called, left behind them.

> Sad as it was to survey the charred remains of what once had passed for prosperity in this nonindustrial region, sadder by far were the people of those counties through which the blue column had slogged on its way to and from the town that now was little more than a scar on the green breast of earth. They had the stunned, unbelieving look of survivors of some terrible natural disaster, such as a five-day hurricane, a tidal wave, or an earth-

quake: with the underlying difference that their grief had been inflicted by human design and was in fact a deliberate product of a new kind of war, quite unlike the one for which they had bargained three years ago, back in that first springtime of secession.[4]

It was indeed hard to comprehend that this destruction was no unavoidable by-product of warfare, but a calculated strategy. It was galling that these bummers took such obvious pleasure in their work and more galling still that they would be hailed as heroes when they returned to Washington for the grand victory parade. Horace Porter described the scene. "And then," he wrote, "came the amusing spectacle of 'Sherman's Bummers' bearing with them the 'spoils of war. . . .' The trophies . . . which appeared in the review consisted of pack mules loaded with turkeys, geese, chickens, and bacon, and here and there a chicken-coop strapped on to the saddle with a cackling brood peering out through the slats. Then came cows, goats, sheep, donkeys, crowing roosters, and in one instance a chattering monkey."[5]

The spectacle was not amusing to the southerners who were the victims of this startlingly cruel concept of warfare. For years after the war, plundered belongings turned up in northern pawn shops, and southerners long charged that the houses of Union officers and chaplains in almost every northern village were filled with stolen gold, pictures, books, clothing, pianos, and silverware, proudly displayed as "confiscated" property.

Not long after Sherman's five days of destruction, word arrived that John Wesley and William's father had died in battle. The boys' mother was devastated. How could the Yankees kill this kind, strong, blue-eyed man, so full of fun and spirit? Unable to accept the fact of his death, Great Grandmother Harris began a daily ritual. Every morning, after breakfast, she would gather the two boys, and they would ride the buckboard the several miles into Meridian—then nothing but a smoking ruin, identifiable as a town only by the chimneys where houses once stood. The little group would drive up to the railroad tracks, and the widow would tell the boys to stay put. Then she would kneel at the edge of the rail, and place her ear just above it to listen for the sounds of the train bringing back her husband.

She never recovered from the blow. Within a few months of her husband's death Great Grandmother Harris was put to bed. Expressing the hope that she would see her husband in heaven, she died several days before the peace of Appomattox.

The Reverend Junius C. Newman, pastor of the Methodist church, had tried in vain to console the widow. Now, he took the boys in, sharing with them the little food available to his family. Sherman's bummers had stolen almost everything they owned, leaving them little more than a few items of furniture and the clothes on their backs. The Union troops had torn up Newman's fences, driven away his cattle, and stolen the food that was stored on his once thriving plantation. Stunned by these events and the desolation that overwhelmed Meridian, Newman began his plans for moving his newly enlarged family to a safer area. The civilian population was almost beyond help. With no place to live and little food to eat, many sought refuge in the shade of trees or in borrowed tents until they rebuilt or migrated to other parts. Newman wondered whether life in Brazil, about which he had read, might not be preferable to this living hell that General Sherman had created.

Thousands of other southerners were considering the same idea as the end of the war approached. They were horrified by the prospect of defeat for the Confederate States of America, and as it became clearer and clearer that defeat was inevitable, despair spread among them. Two days before the surrender of General Lee, one southern lady wrote in her diary: "The war is closing in upon us from all sides. I am afraid there are rougher times ahead than we have ever known yet. . . . nobody seems to doubt it and everybody feels ready to give up hope. There is a complete revulsion in public feeling. No more talk about help from France and England, but all about emigration to Mexico and Brazil."[6]

Birds no longer sang. Defeat had covered the South with the gray palor of hopelessness. The southern landscape was in shambles. Almost every family mourned the loss of at least one relative in the war. Railroads were torn up. Churches and schools were closed. Every bank was insolvent. Homes, farms, and plantations were destroyed. Entire towns and cities were reduced to rubble. The economy had collapsed. Work was at a standstill as rootless men and women, black and white, roamed the countryside.

Soon after the peace, northern tax collectors descended on the South, bent on making the rebels pay for the war. Hodding Carter tells about unscrupulous Yankee agents buying distressed property for resale at huge profits. They were able to buy an estate worth forty thousand dollars for two hundred dollars, one worth fifteen thousand dollars for three hundred dollars, and an entire town (Fernandina, Florida) for ten thousand dollars.[7]

It was insult, as well as poverty and ruin, that oppressed the South. Congress chose to be vindictive toward its conquered countrymen. Having branded 3.5 million southerners as traitors, the legislators were soon deep in debate over how to punish this rather large group of prisoners. They declared 150,000 of the Confederacy's leading citizens guilty without trial and deprived them of the rights of citizenship. The haughty planter was to be taught a lesson in humility. He would have to ask for a pardon before his citizenship would be restored. But for the foremost leaders of the insurrection, there was to be no forgiveness. Only weeks after the surrender at Appomattox, Robert E. Lee, as a gesture of national reconciliation, formally requested a pardon. His request was ignored. Not until 1976—111 years later—was Lee's citizenship posthumously retored. Jefferson Davis fared even worse. The president of the Confederacy was imprisoned like a common criminal, chained, and threatened. It was this particular bit of revenge, perhaps, that most angered the South.

The insults were piled one on top of the other. It was not long before the Yankee press found reason to ridicule even the South's newfound poverty. For example, J. T. Trowbridge, a northern newspaperman, after a postwar trip through the South, wrote: "They are all Rebels here—all Rebels! . . . They are a pitiably poverty-stricken set; there is no money in the place, and scarcely anything to eat. We have for breakfast salt fish, fried potatoes, and treason. Fried potatoes, treason, and salt fish for dinner. At supper the fare is slightly varied, and we have treason, salt fish, fried potatoes, and a little more treason. . . . The war feeling here is like a burning bush with a wet blanket wrapped around it. Looked at from the outside, the fire seems quenched. But just peep under the blanket and there it is, all alive and eating, eating in."[8]

There's little wonder that thousands of southerners began to pack and to plan their exodus to Brazil or Mexico or some other area of the globe. Emigration began to seem like the only escape from an intolerable situation. In 1869 George Washington Keyes, formerly of Montgomery, Alabama, thought about the bloody war and the vindictive peace that followed. From his plantation residence in Brazil he wrote to a friend back in America: "I left the United States because of anarchy which I expected to prevail, poverty that was already at our doors, and the demoralization which I thought and still believe will surely cover the land." Fifty years after the war, Dr. Robert Norris, one of the earlier emigrants to Brazil still felt the same way. When asked by an American visitor to Brazil why he didn't return to the United States, he replied: "You folks made our lives so impossible in the United States that we had to leave. We were welcome here in Brazil. This is our country now and here we are going to stay." Helpless under military occupation and burdened by the psychology of defeat, a sense of guilt, and the economic devastation wrought by the war, many felt they had no choice but to leave. They couldn't simply outwait their conquerors, biding their time until the Yankees just went away and left them alone. They were far too bitter for that.

A popular song in the South after the war gives us a feeling for southern attitudes. Written by Major Innes Randolph, veteran of the Confederate army, the song seems amusing on its face. But the humor masks an undercurrent of the kind of anger it would take to give up almost everything—friends, family, and community—and sail to far-off Brazil or Mexico.

OH, I'M A GOOD OLD REBEL

Oh, I'm a good old Rebel, now that's just what I am.
For this "Fair Land of Freedom" I do not give a damn!

I'm glad I fit against it, I only wish we'd won,
And I don't want no pardon for anything I done.

I hates the Constitution. Their Great Republic, too.
I hates the Freedman's Buro, In uniforms of blue;
I hates the nasty eagle, with all his brag and fuss,
The lyin', thievin' Yankees, I hates 'em wuss and wuss.

I hates the Yankee nation and everything they do.
I hates the Declaration of Independence, too;
I hates the "glorious Union," 'Tis dripping with our blood,
I hates their striped banner, I fit it all I could.

I followed ol Marse Robert for four year, near about,
Got wounded in three places, and starved at Point Lookout;
I cotch the "roomatism," A-campin in the snow,
But I killed a chance o' Yankees, I'd like to kill some mo'.

Three hundred thousand Yankees is still in Southern dust;
We got three hundred thousand before they conquered us;
They died of Southern fever and Southern steel and shot,
I wish they was three million instead of what we got.

I can't take up my musket and fight 'em now no more,
But I ain't agoing to love 'em, now that is certain sure;
And I dont want no pardon for what I was and am,
I won't be reconstructed and I don't care a damn!

I won't be reconstructed! I'm better now than then;
And for a carpetbagger, I don't give a damn;
So I'm off for the frontier, soon as I can go,
I'll prepare me a weapon and start for Mexico.

The colonists made their choice. Rather than stay behind and debate the meaning of "treason" or humbly, hat in hand, await the return of their rights as citizens of the newly reunited United States only to live as exiles in their native land, they closed the gates behind them and headed farther south. Leaving was the one remaining gesture of defiance they could make to the Yankee conqueror.

TWO

Night Is the Beginning and the End

VOLTAIRE has written that historians must play on the dead whatever tricks they deem necessary for their own peace of mind. Over the years, it has served America to minimize the postwar exodus of southerners to Brazil or to dismiss it as a voyage of mad adventurers. Nineteenth-century America chose to believe that only a few participated and that those foolish few were undoubtedly wiped out in the steamy, vermin-infested jungles in the interior of Brazil. Down through the years, short press accounts have appeared, with wildly varying totals of the emigrants, but generally underestimating their number, giving the impression that there were only a few hundred.

Actually, three million people migrated from the former Confederate states in the decades following the Civil War. Most of these southerners moved to sparsely settled lands in western North America, to the larger cities of the North, to Canada, and to Mexico. Exactly how many chose to emigrate to Brazil is uncertain, for crossing national borders entailed fewer formalities than in modern times. T. Lynn Smith can estimate with fair accuracy that twenty thousand Germans emigrated to Brazil after World War II.[1] In the 1860s and 1870s, however, as second-generation Confederado Charles MacFadden pointed out in an interview with PBS television, no one was counting. Few of the southerners had passports; they simply boarded ships and came on down. Not until 1884 did Brazil begin keeping accurate immigration records.

11

Charles Nathan, a longtime resident of Brazil, in the 1870s estimated that about twenty-nine hundred southerners came to Brazil each year from 1867 to 1871. However, he counted only those settlers who entered through the city of Rio de Janeiro. American southerners actually landed in dozens of ports in Brazil. Sources such as the *Brazilian Immigration and Colonization Review* of the Departamento Nacional de Imigração have acknowledged that the United States supplied significant numbers of immigrants to the vast Brazilian nation. A study of available figures, newspaper reports, and personal data gathered from descendants makes it safe to estimate that at least twenty thousand southerners emigrated to Brazil. The descendants of these settlers now number over one hundred thousand, and they are scattered throughout the country.

U.S. historians have little noted the Brazilian migration. Blanche H. C. Weaver commented: "The effort of the Brazilian government to attract immigrants from southern United States in the years immediately following the Civil War has received scant attention. . . . Frequently the entire subject is disposed of in one or two sentences. . . . From the North American side the entire episode is considered a minor detail of the Reconstruction period, seldom mentioned in general accounts."[2] The Brazilian writer Vianna Moog made the event a central part of his classic study of the comparative historical development of the United States and Brazil, *Bandeirantes and Pioneers*. He, too, wonders about this unique case of American emigration. He called it "a blank chapter, so great is the scarcity of positive data about this strange episode, so great the silence about it."[3]

At the time of the exodus, however, emigration fever was widely discussed. Some newspapers imposed a blackout on the event, hoping thus to avoid encouraging the prospective emigrants, but many newspapers in both South and North editorialized against it. Neither approach stemmed the tide. Conversations, letters, diaries, literature, and songs of the time were full of migration sentiment. The emigrants were a cross section of southern society. Most were professional farmers and planters, but others were part-time agriculturists. These included generals, admirals, governors, senators, as well as mechanics, machinists, preachers, and teachers, and even a few freed slaves. Some feared that the exodus would strip the South of its most energetic citizens—its leaders, its engineers, its teachers, and its physicians. Indeed, one group of settlers bound for central Brazil included a large percentage of medical doctors. Twentieth-century newspapers would have labeled it the "brain drain."

Nothing stings the pride of a country more than the fact of emigration. We have seen recent examples of harsh responses by nations to citizens who wish to leave the motherland. Eastern Europe has built a wall to keep them in. No such obstacles impeded the migration of Confederates to other parts of the world, but the movement was looked upon with extreme distaste by the authorities in Washington. Some newspapers described the Confederados as fools. The idea that Americans might actually leave seemed absurd. America was where immigrants came! But the United States was a country welcoming huddled immigrant masses to eastern ports while proud Confederates sailed south, out of the New Orleans back door. The *Charleston Daily News and Courier*, the *New Orleans Times*, the *True Delta and Crescent*, the *Alabama State Journal*, and the *Mobile Daily Register*—all pointed out the folly of migrating to Brazil. And these and other newspapers were quick to pounce with vehemence on the story of the occasional group that returned to the United States. With ethnocentric certitude, one editor railed:

> There arrived at the Central Hotel last night, a party of ladies and gentlemen who left Brazil last month, thoroughly, totally, heartily disgusted with their new homes among the hybrid masses in this overrated, well-flattered country of Brazil. The party is composed entirely of Alabamians . . . eighteen gentlemen and their wives and children. They give affecting and pitiful accounts of the sufferings of many hundreds of deluded Southerners who were lured away from their friends by the tempting offers of the Brazilian adventurers. They represent that there is no regularly organized Government in Brazil—there is no society—but little cultivation among the inhabitants—no laudable ambition—no ways of making money—the people scarcely know the meaning of the word "kindness"—the Ameri-

can citizens live about in huts, uncared for—there is much general dissatisfaction among the emigrants and the whole Brazil representation is a humbug and a farce. The American Consul is in receipt of numerous and constant applications from helpless American citizens to assist them in getting back to their true, rightful country. . . . Dissipate the idea that Alabama is not still a great country—cease dreaming over the unhappy past—say nothing that will assist to keep up political troubles, stay at home, but work, work, work and Alabama will yet be, what she ought to be and can be, a great and glorious country![4]

In contrast, we have the comments of Frank Shippey, one of the early Confederados, who wrote to a friend in New Orleans: "Since the surrender of our armies, I have roamed in exile over the fairest portions of the globe. But it has been reserved for me to find in Brazil that peace which we all, from sad experience, know so well to appreciate. Here, the war worn soldier, the bereaved parent, the oppressed patriot, the homeless and despoiled, can find a refuge from the trials which beset them, and a home not haunted by the eternal remembrance of harrowing scenes of sorrow and of death."[5] The evidence shows that most Confederados survived quite well and were a hardy, adaptable lot. By 1869 a Confederate living in Rio could write to friends in the U.S., "All the Confederates are doing well, perhaps better than they could do in the United States."[6] In a letter to the editor published May 19, 1868, in the *Charleston Mercury*, Colonel Charles Gunter, formerly a prominent cotton grower of Alabama, then living on the banks of the Doce River in Brazil, wrote:

Move here and buy land, which you can do on four year's credit, at twenty-two cents per acre, better than I ever saw anywhere in the United States even in the richest portions of Alabama. With your sons to assist you, you will be as independent in a year as any person need be. Bring with you all tools you can, as yours are generally better than can be bought here. Bring all your household furniture except very heavy articles of wood. Bring as many kinds of seed as you can, fig and grape cuttings. . . . With what means you have don't fear to start. With your furniture, tools and the labor of your sons I should consider you rich. If you can bring any number of such families as your own, I can safely guarantee them homes, and plenty in a land for which Providence has done more than for any other I have ever seen or heard of. (I have almost forgiven our enemies all their wrongs, on account of the better country to which they forced me.) We have here a beautiful place for our village, in the center of rich land, and on a grand river. . . . This is mid-summer, thermometer at 85 ranging through the year from 95 to 65. We are twenty-five miles from the sea, and have a daily breeze from the Atlantic. There are now about twenty families here, and before you can join us, shall have a steamer on the river. Our government is unobjectionable; there is the most perfect freedom of religious worship.

Many of the early settlers wrote back to their homeland with similar sentiments, keeping the migration fever boiling.

The exodus to Mexico, which began even earlier than emigration to Brazil, was far less successful, and the failures in that country provided propaganda for the antiemigrationists. Initially, Mexico seemed so attractive, particularly to the military and political leaders of the Confederacy. Many of these men were still young and ambitious, aware that it might be possible to return to the South and resume their careers when things cooled down. A base in Mexico, just across the border, where the Emperor Maximilian was sure to welcome experienced fighting men, might be the perfect jumping-off place for future activities back in the United States.

Jefferson Davis and some of his generals were not ready to give up when Lee surrendered his armies at Appomattox. Only a month before, Davis had given a fiery speech urging the South to fight on, despite the odds. Some generals wanted to continue guerrilla warfare; one wrote, "We owe it to our manhood, to the memory of the dead, and to the honor of our arms, to remain steadfast to the last."[7] Jefferson Davis received a message from General Wade Hampton that said: "Give me a good force of cavalry and I will take them safely across the Mississippi—and if you desire to go in that direction it will give me great pleasure to escort you. I can bring to your support many strong arms and brave hearts—men who will fight to Texas, and who, if forced from that state, will seek refuge in Mexico."[8] Despite Lee's surrender, Davis knew that there were still more than 150,000 Confederate troops farther west. This force was immobile, however, having been outflanked by the eastward surge of the war. If the armies of Generals Mosby, Shelby, Kirby-Smith, Forrest, and President Zachary Taylor's son Richard B. Taylor could link up in the southwest, the struggle could continue.

Events moved too swiftly for the hotheaded generals. Davis was captured in Georgia, and Taylor and Kirby-Smith were forced to surrender the bulk of their armies. At the last-ditch headquarters of the Confederacy in Marshall, Texas, General Joseph Shelby and the remaining generals met with several Confederate state governors to make plans. The group hesitated for many weeks, debating whether to cross the Rio Grande. They knew that linking their fate with Maximilian's was risky. The French puppet's government was tottering under the strong assault being made upon it by the armies of Benito Juarez. Finally, the group made its decision, and the column marched southward.

A painting of a ceremony hangs today in the dining room of the Fort Duncan Club at Eagle Pass, Texas. It shows General Jo Shelby casting a tattered flag of the Confederacy, the Stars and Bars, into the waters of the Rio Grande. He is surrounded by loyal mounted troopers as a bugler sounds the call. Their heads are bared.

The event is depicted accurately. The Iron Cavalry Brigade, containing some of the Confederate army's finest fighting men, crossed the Rio Grande on July 4, 1865, taking along cannons and supplies, for exile in Mexico. As a last symbolic act in a war in which the Iron Cavalry had distinguished itself, the group refused to surrender, choosing instead to follow the bravest of them all, their leader, Jo Shelby. No behind-the-lines strategist, this general stood with his men where the firing was thickest. He was wounded three times in battle, and miraculously, he survived twenty-three horses shot out from under him. Pride and courage had brought him this far, and he was not disposed to subject his brigade to ignominious surrender. When challenged by Juarist forces on the twelve-hundred-mile route from the border south to Mexico City, Shelby's men fought back furiously, suffering many casualties.

The brigade, still intact and still an organized fighting force, marched into Mexico City in August 1865.

After a private audience with Emperor Maximilian at which Shelby requested and received asylum, the general called a meeting of his troops. He disbanded them, advising them to join one of the projected agricultural colonies being planned by Maximilian for the thousands of Americans that were migrating to his country.

Although fewer Confederates settled in Mexico than in Brazil, more high-ranking southerners chose Mexico. In addition to Shelby, Generals John B. Magruder, Edmund Kirby-Smith (commander-in-chief of the forces of the Trans-Mississippi and almost equal in importance to General Lee), Sterling Price, William P. Hardeman, Cadmus M. Wilcox, Trusten Polk, Hamilton Bee, George Fournoy, Monroe Parsons, and Thomas C. Hindman went to Mexico. So did Governors Henry W. Allen of Louisiana, Isham Harris of Tennessee, and Charles S. Morehead of Kentucky. Former governors Pendleton Murrah and Edward Clark of Texas and the notable Commodore Matthew Fontaine Maury also chose to leave for Mexico.[9] In contrast, Brazil attracted only two Confederates with the rank of general, General W. W. Wood of Mississippi and General A. T. Hawthorne of Texas.

There was good reason for most southerners to prefer Brazil. Whereas most Brazilians welcomed the Confederates, despite their cultural and religious differences, in Mexico only the royalists were glad to see them arrive. The memory of the 1847 war with the United States in which the Mexicans lost over half of their national territory was still fresh, and it fueled a traditional suspicion of their northern neighbors. Moreover, the unrest in Mexico was worsening daily.

It wasn't long before things began to unravel in Mexico. The emperor, with the aid of his newly appointed emigration agent, Commodore Maury, had begun his plan to colonize Mexico with at least fifty thousand Confederates. Maury summoned up his writing talent to recruit emigrants through articles and personal letters back to the States. As one of the experts on life in both Brazil and Mexico, he found an attentive

audience in the southern states. But Mexican colonization efforts were being hampered by the guerrilla warfare in the countryside and the increasing strength of Juarist forces to the north
along the U.S. border.

Juarez was egged on by the government in Washington,
anxious to see the French leave. General Phil Sheridan was
dispatched to patrol the border and the ports of New Orleans
and Mobile to hamper the exodus of the Confederates and their
families, but his net was ineffective. Despite delays, many rode
across the border or took ship to Veracruz, then traveled over-
land to Mexico City. Their stay in Mexico was brief.

The largest settlement of Confederates was at Carlota,
where rich agricultural lands were sold cheaply and several
thousand of the colonists had taken refuge. But in March 1867,
with the withdrawal of royalist troops, the colony was abandoned overnight. The Confederates fled toward the port of
Veracruz either to return to the U.S. or to continue their migration to Brazil, Cuba, Venezuela, or other South American
countries. In many cases the withdrawal was accompanied by
bloodshed.

At sunrise, on June 19, 1867, Maximilian was taken before a firing squad in Querétaro. His death precipitated the
hasty withdrawal from the country of the rest of the Confederate emigrants. Many did not escape. A. F. Rolle describes an
attack on the Confederate colony at Tuxpan, Mexico.

> The colony was destroyed almost overnight. The air thick
> with dust and smoke, the flames from their huts leaping skyward,
> the gunfire deafening them, Tuxpan's terrified immigrants at-
> tempted escape by sea. The countryside bristled with enemy
> guns. With few weapons, supplies, and practically no earth-
> works, the Tuxpan colonists grimly dug hasty defenses along the
> beaches. Their only hope was to put up a delaying action while
> they prepared an escape in their pest-ridden, leaky old scows.
> The situation became progressively more desperate. Some of the
> boats on which the Confederates hoped to escape were captured
> by hostile natives who put the colonists to the torch and threw
> their corpses into the ocean.[10]

This was not a unique incident. It was only one of many en-
counters of the Mexican migration. There's little wonder that

the Confederates in Mexico decided to pull up stakes and head on south to Brazil or back to the United States.

Those who returned were met with a barrage of criticism in the American press. The many Radical Republican newspapers that had sprung up in the South joined in the abuse. Such was the clamor over "foolish returning exiles" and the ridicule heaped on them that many who had long planned their journey to Brazil began to have second thoughts. The fact that General Robert E. Lee vociferously opposed emigration also deterred many.

Even before all of the Confederate naval forces had ended their activities, less than a month after the surrender of the army, General Lee, from his temporary home in Richmond, began his campaign to bind up the nation's wounds. He believed that the best course was to submit completely to the new authority. To set the example for his fellow southerners, on June 13, 1865, he applied for his pardon. He hoped that the South would freely accept its new government, for the alternative was anarchy, extended military rule, and added punishment for the ex-Confederates—especially Jefferson Davis and the other leaders.

It concerned Lee that there was so much talk about emigration to Brazil and Mexico. Southerners were organizing colonization societies in each state to promote emigration on a vast level. Brazilian fever, as the newspapers called it, threatened to take the South's best people, a loss the region could ill afford. Lee believed that southerners should stay home and begin the work of rebuilding. When Emperor Maximilian of Mexico tendered his formal invitation to Confederates to settle in his country, the general wrote: "I do not know how far emigration to another land will conduce to their prosperity. Although prospects may not now be cheering, I have entertained the opinion that, unless prevented by circumstances or necessity, it would be better for them and the country if they remained at their homes and shared the fate of their respective states."[11]

His words had their effect. The opinion of General Lee, the hero of the South, carried much weight. He was, in that time immediately after the war, the symbol of the South. Not until later was Jefferson Davis to reach this level of veneration; he had first to endure a martyrdom of maltreatment in northern prisons. Davis was if anything an encouragement to leave, for he himself had been captured while attempting to flee to Mexico. Now that he was imprisoned at Fortress Monroe, he was muzzled. Only Lee was free to speak out, and the general was influential. As his secretary, Colonel Charles Marshall, wrote:

> General Lee set to work to use his great influence to reconcile the people of the South to the hard consequences of their defeat, to inspire them with hope, to lead them to accept, freely and frankly, the government that had been established by the result of the war, and thus relieve them from military rule. . . . The advice and example of General Lee did more to incline the scale in favor of a frank and manly adoption of that course of conduct which tended to the restoration of peace and harmony than all the Federal garrisons in all the military districts.[12]

Lee was a practical man. To the questions of how to feed and house the inhabitants of a devastated South and how to endure the continued domination of the northern forces, he gave direct answers. "I am sorry," he wrote,

> to hear that our returned soldiers cannot obtain employment. Tell them they must all set to work, and if they cannot do what they prefer, do what they can. Virginia wants all their aid, all their support, and the presence of all her sons to sustain and recuperate her. They must therefore put themselves in a position to take part in her government, and not be deterred by obstacles in their way. There is much to be done which they only can do.[13]

To the governor of Virginia he wrote: "They should remain, if possible, in the country; promote harmony and good feeling, qualify themselves to vote and elect to the State and general legislatures wise and patriotic men, who will devote their abilities to the interest of the country and the healing of all dissensions. I have invariably recommended this course since the cessation of hostilities, and have endeavoured to practice it myself."[14]

And some of the press took up the drumbeat, supporting the general in his stand. The word was given: migration was to be considered unmanly and unpatriotic. Everyone did not agree, and the work of colonization continued, but at a considerably reduced level of enthusiasm. Jefferson Davis himself, while he was imprisoned, petitioned the federal authorities to allow his family to emigrate overseas. After his release, however, Davis joined the opposition to emigration. "Because the *mass of our people* could not go, the few who were able to do so were most needed to sustain the others in the hour of a common adversity," he wrote.[15]

Despite this opposition from newspapers, politicians, and even the most revered heroes of the recent struggle, thousands of southerners succumbed to the lure of Brazil. The fear of the changes the Yankee triumph would bring and the strong desire to maintain their own way of life gave many the deep commitment necessary to leave the South for an unfamiliar and distant country in Latin America. Unlike the high-ranking Confederates who darted into Mexico seeking a temporary haven from which to return and reestablish themselves, those who left for Brazil expected never to see their homeland again. Martha Steagall knew she would never go back home to Gonzales, Texas, and so she insisted on taking her parlor piano with her when she embarked on the thirty-day voyage to her new country.

The Americans who left for Brazil went as settlers, hoping to quietly maintain the society they had known all their lives. Few Confederates of high rank made the journey. Brazil attracted no state governors or highly placed Confederate political figures. But more Confederates migrated to Brazil than to Mexico, for Brazil had more to offer to a permanent settler.

To learn what motivated this unique migration from an America just plunging into the Industrial Age, one has to look beyond economic statistics to the more human aspects of sectional pride, hate of the wartime enemy and the instinctive urge to preserve southern cultural values. The choice was wide. There were other countries in the world, many nearby, that offered sanctuary. But Brazil held a place in Confederate hearts through popular books on the subject, widely read in the South prior to the conflict.

At first glance, Brazil seemed, at best, a secondary pros-

pect for colonization. It still had slavery—and this was attractive to many of the Confederados—but was in the process of
ridding itself of the practice. The importation of slaves had
been outlawed in 1850. In any case, had the desire to continue
owning slaves been the only motive for the Brazil migration,
southerners would have found it much easier to settle in nearby
Cuba, only one day's journey from Florida, than in a land five-
thousand miles away. Slavery existed in Cuba until 1886 and in
Brazil until 1888. And from the very first, the migrants had
been informed that Brazil possessed "negro equality," but that
did not discourage them.[16] Better to live among Negro peers
than among Yankees.

If the emigrants were spurred only by the glint of economic
opportunity in going to Brazil, they were misled. Economic
opportunity, especially for agriculturists, was nearer their own
backyard. Land in the West was selling at $1.25 an acre, the
price set by Congress. Compared to the net cost of colonizing in
Brazil, moving to the western part of the United States made
more economic sense. The passage of the Homestead Act in
1862 ensured low-cost (even free) western lands to settlers.
Confederados ignored the fertile topsoil and the mineral resources of the West, however, in favor of a faraway country's
unknown soil and primitive farm-to-market transportation system. They also ignored the attraction of common language,
similar customs and heritage. They were enveloped in the
memory of the war and resentful of the proximity of the Yankees. Their plan was to isolate themselves and set up communities that treasured southern ways—a confederacy of the
mind.

Brazil attracted Confederates for many other reasons. Because of its size it offered a variety of climates including warm-
to-moderate weather similar to that of the southern states from
which they came. It had plenty of available sugarcane- and
cotton-growing land, cheap labor, and religious and political
tolerance.

Brazil's slavery was being phased out peacefully, if fitfully.
Understandably the migrants were interested in the methods
employed in Brazil to eliminate the practice. There was no sign

of violent confrontation or civil war. The debate there cen-
tered, not on the opening of new lands for slavery, but on when
to cease it and how much indemnity should be paid the
slaveholders.

The Confederate planters admired the trappings of Dom
Pedro II's empire, similar in many respects to their own plantation society back in the South. Brazilian palaces and their
evidence of conspicuous consumption were first cousin to the
life-style of the more prosperous southern plantations. This
atmosphere offered hope that their way of life might be preserved.

All these factors persuaded southerners to move to Brazil,
but perhaps they also made the journey out of instinctive need
to change, to move their way of life to the atmosphere of
another culture. Perhaps change would eliminate the feeling of
guilt—the buried guilt of slaveholders, of warriors, of those who
urged their sons to their death in battle. One of the changes
most evident in the Confederados of my youth (the 1920s and
1930s) was their belief in tolerance among the races. This they
had acquired from the Brazilians. Almost uniquely in the
world, Brazil has a long-standing harmonious relationship
among its races. Over time most of the emigrants and all of
their descendants came around to the Brazilian way of thinking
on this subject. Lawrence Durrell has written: "Journeys, like
artists, are born and not made." And he adds, "and the best of
them lead us not only outwards in space, but inwards as well."[17]

By 1867 one Brazilian newspaper reported that the Confederados were so numerous that they seemed to be living on
every block of Rio de Janeiro, already a large city of 500,000
residents. Even after Washington offered amnesty to most
southerners seven years after the end of the war, the emigrés
stayed put. They added their distinctive and, to the Brazilians,
sometimes baffling cultural trappings to Brazil's immigrant
melting pot.

So well did they blend into their Brazilian setting that, as
far as the United States was concerned, they disappeared al-
together.

Oddly, it is the tourists who have recently rediscovered

the supposedly failed colony at remote Santarém in the humid
Amazon. The observant Stephen Birnbaum, author of a best-
selling tourism guide *South America, 1983,* after exploring the
Amazon, wrote:

> This city of 150,000 was settled in 1865 by residents of South
> Carolina and Tennessee who fled the Confederacy where slavery
> was abolished. Brazil permitted slavery for only 23 years after
> their arrival, but the Southerners still prospered and built a town
> that has become an important trading center. It now serves as a
> supply center for miners, gold prospectors, rubber tappers,
> Brazil-nut gatherers, and the jute and lumber industries. Several
> bars display the Confederate flag, and you still occasionally meet
> the settlers' descendants, who mixed with the multiracial Brazil-
> ians and have names like Jose Carlos Calhoun.[18]

Santarém is located in one of the world's most isolated and
underdeveloped areas, where even Brazilians have historically
feared to tread, resisting their own government's efforts to
populate the region. The city is quaint in a way that seems to
appeal to the more adventuresome tourists. Crisscrossed with
unpaved streets, it is reached mainly by boat on the fabled
Amazon River. It swelters in the midst of the twenty-two-
hundred-mile-long malarial Amazon jungle. To enter qualifies
one as an explorer, and many an intrepid European or American has met his Waterloo in this area where the Rio Tapajós
empties into the mighty Amazon. Even President Theodore
Roosevelt, a rugged outdoorsman, failed in his attempt to master the jungle on his 1914 exploration of the area. He fell
victim to its diseases and never regained his health after that
expedition.

Much more hospitable is Brazil's land mass to the south,
but it should be noted that Birnbaum's popular guidebook has
yet to discover the vastly larger settlements of Confederates in
the southern part. One would think that even the name *Americana* would attract the attention of the most casual American
historical researcher. Moreover, it is Brazil's leading cotton
textile city, in the highly industrially developed state of São
Paulo only a short ride over a four-lane highway from the international airport. It is something, at least, that Santarém has
been rediscovered.

The saga of the Amazon settlement begins with the arrival in Rio de Janeiro in 1835 of Fountaine E. Pitts of Tennessee. He worked as a missionary, traveling about the country for five years, until he was reassigned to the U.S. Deeply impressed by his experiences there, Pitts never tired of recounting to his son the marvels of the country and the economic opportunities, especially in the tropical portion. After the war, Pitts's son, Dr. Joseph Pitts joined with Major Lansford Warren Hastings to establish a colony of fellow southerners in the Amazon.

Hastings was a restless adventurer, well known throughout the United States for his *Emigrant's Guide to Oregon and California* (1845), which persuaded many to cross the Rocky Mountains to settle in the Far West. He had been involved in the highly publicized California-bound expedition that had met disaster at the Donner Pass while attempting a midwinter crossing of the mountain range, and he was a member of the California Constitutional Convention of 1849. During the Civil War, he encouraged the Confederate plan to capture Arizona and New Mexico in the hope of providing southerners access to the Pacific Ocean. The plan failed to gain needed support from the Richmond government, however.

Hastings had married into the Confederacy. An Ohioan by birth, he wed a young lady from Alabama, whose father was from Virginia and whose mother came from Venezuela. He took up the Confederate cause, defining the Civil War as a struggle between the Yankees and the Confederates to control the western territories of the United States.

The most tenacious of the colonizers, Hastings would set sail four times for Brazil. On his first trip he traveled over that country for six months, surveying various colony sites. He then left, with a group of colonists from New Orleans on a ship that foundered on the coast of Cuba. The survivors scattered, mostly to Mexico. His third trip also ended prematurely when smallpox broke out on board and the ship turned back. Forty-six passengers died from the disease.

Undaunted, and possessed by his dream of colonization, he embarked on his fourth trip, suffering his final misfortune. At a stop in St. Thomas, the ship was seized and sold by creditors, stranding the southerners for a month until they could obtain passage to their new Amazon home. At St. Thomas his personal saga ends. Worn out and frustrated, he contracted yellow fever and died without seeing the results of his persistent colonization efforts.

The passionate words he left in his book, *Emigrant's Guide to Brazil*, were to be his epitaph, and the descriptions of life in the romantic, dreamlike Amazon continued to lure Confederates to the Amazon for many years.

> Who can picture, who can paint nature as here exhibited? With wonder, admiration and reverential awe, one may contemplate the vastness with which he finds himself here surrounded, the profusion of nature's bounties, and sublimity of scenery, but to describe them, to picture them as they are, is beyond the scope of human capacity. Here we behold the great Amazon, by far the largest river in the world, located in the center of the world, with its vast tributaries, affording more than ten thousand miles of uninterrupted, fluvial navigation; extending from the ocean to the Andes, and from the Orinoco to the La Plata, embracing more than two million square miles, teeming with animal and vegetable life; a world of eternal verdure and perennial spring, of whose grandeur and splendor it is impossible to speak in fitting terms.[19]

It is easy to see how a man capable of writing so eloquently could persuade others to follow him into the Amazon jungles, and follow him they did.

Most of the colonists had a good idea of what to expect and came prepared for the new life. There were many sources of information, including the following advertisement:

EMIGRATION TO BRAZIL!

> Notice to members of the Pioneer Colony of Major Hastings. Members of the Colony will take notice that the Colony will sail from Mobile, Ala., on the *1st Day* of December, next. A commodious sailing ship of ample tonnage with comfortable accommodations for at least 500 passengers will be provided. Heads of families and single persons will pay $30 each; other members of families over 12, will pay $20 each; and children between 2 and 12, $10 each; which payment will be made in gold coin. Families will be allowed one ton, and single persons 200 pounds of freight, free of charge.

The present destination of the Colony is the City of Pará, on the Amazon, its ultimate location, on a tributary of that river between five and ten degrees latitude. Length of voyage 2000 miles, sailing time about three weeks.

Planters should take their farming utensils, mechanics their tools. Families should take tents and all should provide themselves with provisions for about six months.

Others desiring to become members of this Colony can do so by applying to Major Hastings at No. 40 North Joachim St., Mobile, Ala., B. J. Duncan, Esq., Broad St., Selma, Ala., or Dr. J. W. Keyes, Market St., Montgomery, Ala.[20]

Another good source of information were the articles of Matthew Fontaine Maury, which were widely circulated in southern newspapers. A scientist and explorer, Maury was excited about the economic possibilities of Amazonian Brazil. He was also well informed. In one book, for example, he described the great South American river in terms southern readers could understand. "The Amazon," he wrote, "reminds us of our Mississippi. . . . Its climate is an everlasting summer and its harvest perennial."[21] Picture, if you will, the conditions in 1867 when an intrepid little band of southerners sailed five hundred miles up this river in search of refuge from the Yankees.

Not all the members of Hastings's group were practical people of substance. There were a fair number of barroom loafers along for the adventure. These vagabonds, once they discovered the availability of cheap rum, abandoned themselves to their habit. Some prospective settlers were simply unsuited for colonization. They knew little about farming and had not properly prepared themselves for the adventure into the wilds of tropical Brazil. Some said they had not been told that tools were hard to acquire and so had not brought with them the necessities of farming life. Others complained about the arrangements their sponsors had made. Promised roads to plantation sites had not been finished. Food supplies were inadequate and the Brazilian food was strange looking. All the pioneers struggled to adapt to the alligators, the climate, the soil, and the jungle. They blamed Hastings; they blamed the Brazilian government.

Americans have sometimes singled out this expedition to

the Amazon as the prime example of Confederate foolishness. In the summer of 1869, several dozen settlers, offered transport on U.S. navy ships, decided to return to the United States. The press responded with articles claiming that the Amazon expedition had ended in disaster, but this was not exactly the truth. Although some left, many continued to arrive, more than replacing those who went back, and the little colony soon grew to two hundred residents. Despite the early difficulties, many emigrés settled down, adjusted to their surroundings, and prospered in the humid, colorful Amazon, raising cotton and sugarcane and eating the plentiful tropical fruits and vegetables. Some of the successful settlers tried to set the record straight. Dr. Pitts wrote from Valley Home, Brazil, to the *Mobile Daily Register,* denying that the colony had failed and insisting that the group was in fine condition and doing well. He added: "I have planted corn in January and raised a fine crop, and have planted three times since—and will have an abundance to do me. I have sugar cane, cotton, pumpkins, squash, five kinds of sweet potatoes, Irish potatoes, cornfield peas, snap beans, butter beans, ochre, tomatoes and a fine chance of tobacco. I have made enough to live well on and am better pleased than ever. I have a great variety of fruits on my place."[22] Mrs. N. F. White of the same colony near Santarém was equally enthusiastic in a letter she wrote sixteen months later to the *Nashville Union and Dispatch.* She and her husband had prospered in the manufacture of rum and molasses, and they lacked only the "ordinary institutions of society." She reported that future prospects were bright, for good families were arriving and setting up.[23]

Judge Mendenhall, Hastings's father-in-law, took over the explorer's tract of land near Santarém and in time developed it into a model, prosperous plantation. Many others—including the Emmett, Dobbins, Jennings, Henington, Vaughan, Wallace, and Riker families—made a go of it, too. R. H. Riker had been a railroad president back in South Carolina. His son David married a Brazilian lady from Ceará, raising fourteen children. By 1910, with the aid of his large family, he had acquired vast landholdings, including a rubber plantation with

twenty-five thousand trees. R. J. Henington was a Methodist
minister and plantation owner, and Arch Dobbins was a former
plantation supervisor. These two, together with Riker and R. J.
Rhome were role models for the rest of the group. All their
ventures in the Amazon seemed to succeed well, for they had
come with both working capital and experience.[24]

Nearby Brazilians, watching the Confederates set up their
plantations, noted their modern agricultural techniques and
copied them. Today, these Brazilian farms stand out and are
recognized as quite advanced over the traditional, primitive
planting techniques in the rest of the Amazon area. Prior to the
Confederate colonization, the area had not used the plow,
spade, harrow, or rake.[25]

In 1874 Henington took a vacation trip back to the
United States, visiting the site of his abandoned Mississippi
plantation. In the U.S. the busy parson-planter appealed to the
Methodists to send ministers to the Amazon area. He asked
them to take advantage of the North American presence there
to spread the faith. But his request was denied and he returned.
He lived out his years in Brazil, maintaining contact with the
southerners in other areas of the country and exchanging news
and agricultural information by mail with members of the São
Paulo colony far to the south.

Back in Americana my mother's family would occasionally
catch sight of one of these hardy, high-booted Amazonian
Confederados down for a visit. They traveled about the country
as their holdings increased, and many in their old age were
financially comfortable, even though susceptible to the economic ups and downs of the Amazon region. Rubber and sugar
were their most profitable crops. Clement Jennings, whose
prosperity was typical, was in 1929 the owner and operator of a
two-thousand-acre ranch just outside of Santarém.

But the settlers tended to make their money and move to
town to enjoy it. The original Hastings settlement has long
since been abandoned, and little more than gravestones remain
to memorialize the southerners' tenure. The abandonment in a
way testifies to the success of the transplantation of Confederates to Brazil, for the southerners have blended into the Brazil-

ian population in the Amazon. Such assimilation is difficult to achieve. In my sixteen years in the foreign service, I have seen hundreds of American diplomats try to transplant themselves for a mere two-year stay in a foreign land. Many of them have barely made it through their tours. Even though these diplomats—unlike the Confederados—were expensively housed, some in baronial surroundings, they seemed lost, unable to adapt. Few of them learned the language, and almost none understood the culture of the country they were living in.

In 1940 the *Saturday Evening Post*, which then had a massive circulation, decided to put to rest once and for all the vague stories that were circulating about United States citizens emigrating to Brazil. The passage of time had made the record rather fuzzy. James E. Edmonds, who was sent to Brazil to do the piece, explained that his marching orders were: "What about those Secessionists who settled in Brazil?"[26]

It was a difficult assignment. As Vianna Moog commented: "Little did the journalist know what the Amazon jungle does to marks of civilization. . . . of the old churches and dwellings not one stone is left upon another, for the ant, that great collaborator with the jungle, takes it upon herself to pulverize all ruins."[27] Edmonds soon discovered this ability of the jungle to cover man's tracks, swallowing up whole houses and other plantation buildings after just a few years' abandonment.

But miraculously—for it was 1940, seventy-three years after the Confederates had arrived—the writer ran across David Riker, one of the original colonists. He was living in retirement in Santarém with his Brazilian wife and his many children. He told Edmonds that only he, his brother, and one of the Confederado wives still survived from the original group. He spent his days on his veranda, reading his Bible and watching the river roll by. He still had his Confederate officer's sword. He told Edmonds: "I'm glad I stayed on. God has been good to me. My sons are good sons, my daughters are good daughters. My wife is good and true. We lack for nothing we ought to have. How many can say the same?"[28]

THREE

Noah's Ark

THE pioneers who settled the western United States formed wagon trains for which they chose experienced leaders. Likewise, settlers bound for Brazil soon found that colonization groups offered the safest and most economical means of traveling to their new country. The first step in organizing such groups was to reconnoiter the land to be settled. Those who had sufficient funds simply boarded ship and visited the countries that they were interested in, but most advance scouts were sponsored by groups of people interested in emigration.

A few southerners had moved to Brazil prior to the war and had written letters, telling of the bountiful land, its warm climate, and the probability that cotton could be grown successfully there. The South already knew much about Brazil through the books by Matthew Fontaine Maury and others who had explored the country many years before and had written scholarly works on the subject. But southern colonizers needed more up-to-date knowledge and they set about obtaining it in a systematic fashion.

Soon there were colonization societies with thousands of members. They dispatched emissaries to many nations, including Brazil, Mexico, the Caribbean countries, and to other areas of the United States to gather economic, agricultural, and cultural data and to negotiate with political leaders for inducements to immigration. The output of these early advance scouts was remarkable, resulting in several erudite books that were

surprisingly accurate, considering the difficulties in getting
about in the mid-1860s.

The best-known group organized for the purpose of finding
locations for settlement both in the United States and overseas
was the Southern Colonization Society, formed shortly after
the war under the leadership of Major Joseph Abney of
Edgefield, South Carolina. Abney, after viewing the devastation in nearby Columbia, a once beautiful city that was burned
to the ground during the war, wrote in a letter published in the
Edgefield Advertiser, October 11, 1865:

> The future is enveloped in clouds and darkness, and we were less
> than men if we made no efforts for the preservation of our
> families and to avert the manifold dangers that lie in the
> way. . . . hunger and starvation and madness and crime will run
> through our borders. . . . being assured that vast numbers of our
> friends who are destitute of good farming lands, and now also
> destitute of labor, and yet are embarrassed with debt, must be
> brought to beggary unless they exchange their accustomed habi-
> tations for a more genial clime and more fruitful soil, it is our
> purpose to form a Southern Colonization Society.

At the society's first meeting on August 21, 1865, the
members considered the areas to be examined prior to emigration. "It was resolved to send two or more Agents with as little
delay as practicable to explore the Southern and Western Territories of the United States and especially the great Empire of
Brazil, to ascertain what inducements they might offer for the
immigration of our people, and, in the event of a favorable
report, to make all necessary arrangements for the procurement
of lands, and for the establishment of a good and permanent
settlement there."¹ The Edgefield group formed a committee to
scour up funds for Dr. Hugh G. Shaw and Major Robert
Meriwether, whom they appointed as scouts.

By October 30, Shaw and Meriwether had arrived in Rio
de Janeiro on the steamer *North America.* On May 2, 1866, the
results of their survey were published in the *Edgefield Advertiser*
in a lengthy report that was picked up by other publications in
the South through the exchanges network. (This system, used

to this day by the smaller, grass-roots newspapers of America, provides for the systematic exchange of a newspaper's issues with other newspapers to ensure the rapid, wide distribution of items of interest.)

Another of the emisaries sent to explore the land of Brazil for prospective settlers was General William Wallace Wood of Mississippi, a lawyer and the editor of the *Natchez Free Trader*. He represented four Mississippi counties and nineteen colonization associations. In all, a total of eleven thousand families were depending on Wood to find them a home.

He sailed on the *Montana* in August 1865 without a passport. Wood joined scouts from seven other states. The general's group consisted of James H. Warner, a surgeon from Tennessee; W. C. Kernan of Florida, an architect; J. P. Wesson of Tennessee, dentist; Robert L. Brown of Alabama, plantation owner; and two American residents of São Paulo, Major Ernest Street, a civil engineer, and Henry Snell, who would act as interpreter and advisor on conditions in Brazil. It was a knowledgeable, energetic group of fact finders.

Later they were joined by Dr. James McFadden Gaston, an aristocratic surgeon from Columbia, South Carolina, who in 1866 wrote a book on the subject, entitled *Hunting a Home in Brazil*. Gaston was representing another South Carolina organization, but the Brazilian government also appointed him liaison among all the other scouts, as well. He coordinated all the groups so that they would not stumble over one another.

So numerous were the searching parties that they found themselves encountering each other out on the hunt, and sometimes negotiating for the same tract of potential cotton-growing land. But the memory of shared hard times in the South brought out the best in them, and they worked cooperatively in most cases. Over a dozen groups were exploring along the coast and into some portions of the interior of the state of São Paulo. The Brazil scouts included Warren Hastings, General A. T. Hawthorne, Frank McMullen, William Bowen, Colonel M. S. McSwain, Charles Gunter, the Reverend Ballard Dunn, Gaston, Wood, Dr. John H. Blue, Meriwether, Shaw,

Warner, Wesson, Brown, Kernan, Barr, Chaffie, and Sparks. Dozens of others scouted the land on their own, sending back reports through the exchanges press network in the South.

Welcoming crowds, extending for three blocks, shouted "Long live the Confederados," at dockside receptions of these scouting groups. Brazilians vied for the privilege of entertaining them, and Wood, a handsome man with a martial bearing, was the highlight of Brazil's social season. "Balls and parties and serenades were our nightly accompaniment and whether in town or in the country it was one grand unvarying scene of life, love and seductive friendship," the general recounted.[2] Emperor Dom Pedro met them personally, and bands played "Dixie." In cities, large and small, parades and cheering crowds greeted this advance legion representing Brazil's future citizens. Some predicted as many as a hundred thousand ex-Confederates would soon migrate to this land of the Southern Cross. Brazil was at war with Paraguay, and the military put on a show for General Wood's benefit, showing him around the war front and honoring him with grand receptions.

By the time General Wood returned to the United States the emperor had appointed him commissioner of emigration to Brazil (the same title that Emperor Maximilian had bestowed on Commodore Maury). Southern newspapers noted his return to New York aboard the *South America* on January 25, 1866, and printed summaries of his report encouraging emigration to Brazil. Wood undertook a speaking tour and wrote a short book, *Ho! For Brazil.*[3]

Dr. Gaston was kept busy scouting for his own group and coordinating the other scouts. The former Confederate army surgeon disagreed with General Robert E. Lee's opinion that southerners should not emigrate, and he lost no time before heading south to investigate. Within two months of the surrender of the Army of Northern Virginia, he was on a ship bound for Brazil. There he hoped to get a good accounting of the "soil, climate, production, people and the government." On his forty-first birthday, December 27, 1865, he wrote in his diary that he had reached a crossroads in his life. He had decided to start over in a different world with his wife and six children. He noted the shock of cutting his ties with the United States, but, his confidence rising, he believed that success lay ahead if he settled in Brazil.[4]

Gaston covered the land by train, canoe, mule, and on foot. He studied the port of Santos, noting approvingly that it was deep enough to handle even the largest ships of the time. It was just the place to export the cotton that Confederates would someday grow on plantations with access to this port.

He agreed with General Wood that the best areas for raising cotton seemed to be at Araraquara, Jaú, and Limeira, and he was concerned that Wood had already reserved the same lands by a contract with the Brazilian government, to be held for immigrants from the seven states that Wood represented. Gaston described the soil of the Jaú region lovingly, remarking that it stuck to his shoes when it was wet like the black dirt of southern Mississippi. He found the people there to be healthy, with no cases of malaria reported.[5] As it turned out, the Jaú area proved unsuitable for cotton cultivation but fine for coffee. Grandfather Harris's coffee plantation lay right in the middle of these old cotton lands.

Gaston visited coastal areas including Bertioga and Períque, near Santos. Períque had ensured its place in history when it was captured in 1850 by elements of the British navy who were trying to stop the importation of slaves from Africa. Gaston had an abiding interest in the economics of slavery and noted that a slave could be bought at half the price formerly charged in the U.S.

On one occasion he tried to interest the Brazilian government in a plan to use the cotton-growing expertise of the freed U.S. slaves. He advised the Brazilian government to encourage the former slaves to emigrate to Brazil and then to employ the freedmen as supervisors on the cotton plantations. After some study, the government rejected the plan as unwise, fearing that the freed slaves would incite the Brazilian abolitionists to demand a faster end to the peculiar institution in their country.

Among the people Gaston encountered in his travels were the Whitakers of Rio Claro, who had emigrated many years earlier from England. They gave Gaston friendly assistance, offering mules to transport the advance party. These trans-planted Britishers were to have as their neighbors Lieutenant Colonel Joseph Whitaker, late of the Confederate Army. Known as Ol' Joe Whitaker, the former officer became a wealthy grower of Georgia rattlesnake watermelons in Americana. The Confederados introduced this sweet fruit to Brazil and before long were selling many freightcar loads of the big thumping melons throughout the country.

Ol' Joe whose name became Brazilianized as José, was sometimes confused with José Maria Whitaker, a descendant of the British Whitakers, who later became the Averell Harriman of Brazil. Throughout his long life, he moved in and out of cabinet-level government positions including secretary of the treasury. The British family intermarried with Confederates in the area, and the grandson of the old political figure, Christiano Whitaker is currently consul at the Brazilian consulate in New York City.

As for General Wood, he seems to have lost interest in the Brazil settlement scheme. After reading criticism of his plans in the newspapers, he suffered a change of heart and settled in the United States, becoming an attorney in Adams County, Mississippi. "Sic transit gloria Braziliensis," commented one of the critics.[6]

Among others who declined to move to Brazil was Andrew McCullom of Ellendale Plantation, Terrebonne Parish, Louisiana, who had done his own scouting. He was rich enough to finance his own expedition but could not summon the anger necessary to emigrate.

Those who did decide to leave for Brazil wasted no time. Many were barely surviving in the midst of the South's continuing postwar desolation, and they were impelled by the pressing need to settle their families and establish their new farms. The societies formed groups ranging in size from one hundred to four hundred, chartered ships, and transported the settlers directly to their destination.

In the early days following the conclusion of the war few knew clearly what lay ahead for them in Brazil, and they preferred to travel in groups. As time passed, it became evident that in traveling from New Orleans to Rio de Janeiro, the Confederates were going from one sophisticated large city to another. It became common for single men, families, or small groups to simply book passage on Brazil-bound ships. They could still join one of the forming colonies after they arrived at the starting point, Rio de Janeiro, prior to setting out for the interior. The latter part of 1867 through 1868, however, was the era of group migration. Ships crammed to the gunwales with up to four hundred emigrants and their scant belongings began arriving at Rio de Janeiro.

Emperor Dom Pedro had done much to encourage Confederate immigration. He had his agents meet with prospective colonizers and opened immigration offices at the Brazilian embassy in Washington and the consulate in New York City. Dom Pedro subsidized the settlers' ship passage and saw to it that a bureaucracy was in place for receiving them. Arriving settlers were given free temporary accommodations in an immigrants' hotel in Rio de Janeiro. One diary records the palatial setting:

Rows of Imperial palms stood at each side of the walk which led from the gate to the steps of the building. We saw, on each side, large marble basins where fountains had once played—marble benches, beneath vine-covered arbors. Gay and beautiful flowers, growing in tasteful beds. We passed up the marble steps of the building—this edifice had a piazza, and met the landlord Colonel Broome, who greeted us warmly. He had been a Confederate officer. He showed us our apartments, which contained neat furniture, light iron bedsteads and washstands—all painted green. There were table and chairs sufficient. We soon unpacked and made ourselves comfortable. The rooms were beautifully papered, some with frescoed and gilded ceilings. We could hear the exclamations of delight from the young people [Confederados] who roamed about the grounds. They were in ecstasies—rolled on the grass and dashed about, through the arbors and among the flowers. . . . We were a happy band of emigrants—felt we had reached a place of rest, among kind, generous people, who gave us a welcome we did not expect—food much better than on our ship—not really better, but prepared in a way to make it more palatable. At a trifling cost, we had plenty of fruit. . . . We received many visits from Brazilians and Brazilianized Americans.[7]

Julia Keyes gave a detailed accounting of the inducements
Dom Pedro offered to immigrants.

> The Government of Brazil will sell lands in any of its colonies,
> or in the localities that the emigrants prefer; and will give them
> gratuitous transport from Rio de Janeiro to the seaport to which
> they wish to proceed.
>
> On the choice of the lands and the respective measurement
> being made, the definite deeds to the property shall be delivered
> to them upon payment of the price of the sale of one or two reis
> for each of 52.5 square feet.
>
> The owners of lands purchased from the state are subject to
> the following onus. (1) To cede the land necessary for roads.
> (2) To give free transit to their neighbors, to the public road,
> town or port of embarkation. (3) To allow the taking away of
> needed water. (4) To subject the discovery of any mines to the
> legislation governing the case.
>
> Naturalization: Emigrants who purchase lands and establish
> themselves in Brazil can become citizens, after two years of
> residence. On application, however, to the legislature they can
> obtain dispensation from this lapse of time and may be natu-
> ralized soon after their arrival.
>
> A declaration made before the municipal chamber, or the
> justice of peace, mentioning the native country, the age and
> condition are the formalities required to enable the applicants to
> obtain gratuitously, the naturalization papers, after making oath
> of fidelity to the constitution and the laws of the Empire.
>
> Naturalized citizens are exempt from military service, but are
> subject to that of the national guard of the municipality to
> which they belong. They enjoy all the rights and privileges
> conferred by the constitution, except those of being a deputy, a
> minister of state, or the Regent of the Empire.
>
> Foreigners enjoy in Brazil all the civil rights granted to na-
> tives. They have also full liberty in the exercise of any industry
> not prejudicing another party; inviolable asylum in their houses;
> guarantee of their property, whether material or intellectual;
> complete toleration in religious matters; inviolability of the
> postal correspondence and gratuitous primary education.
>
> The government of Brazil is stable. Its laws and authorities
> protect all without distinction or classes; and the distribution of
> civil and criminal justice is made with equality.[8]

Such liberal inducements enhanced the already favorable
opinions of Dom Pedro among southerners. It was no secret

that Brazil and its emperor had sympathized with the Confederates during the Civil War. While officially maintaining neu-
trality, Dom Pedro helped the Confederacy whenever possible.
Confederate ships running the Yankee blockade sometimes
darted into Brazilian ports when pursued. On one occasion the
North retaliated by invading a Brazilian harbor to capture a
Confederate blockade runner—an incident that strained relations but was settled amicably after the war.

Southerners reciprocated the emperor's good wishes. His
standing in the South was reflected in a poem that appeared
March 18, 1866, in the *New Orleans Picayune* newspaper:

> Oh, give me a ship with sail and with wheel
>   And let me be off to happy Brazil
> Home of the sunbeam—great kingdom of heat,
>   With woods evergreen and snake forty feet!
> Land of the diamond—bright nation of pearls,
>   With monkeys aplenty, and Portuguese girls!
>
> Oh give me a ship with sail and with wheel,
>   And let me be off to happy Brazil!
> I yearn to feel her perpetual spring,
>   And shake by the hand Dom Pedro her king,
> Kneel at his feet—call him, "My Royal Boss!"
>   And receive in return, "Welcome Old Hoss!"

By 1876 the personable sovereign had become a press celebrity.
He was guest of honor at the national Centennial Celebration
held in Philadelphia. There he presented the United States a
gift of São Paulo marble, which now forms a part of the massive
Washington monument in the nation's capital.

One southerner who was convinced of the advantages
Brazil had to offer was the Reverend Ballard Dunn. "After
procuring permission to travel from [his] new masters" (the
Yankees), he took passage on a little schooner, the *Valiant,* and
set off for Rio de Janeiro. He carried introductory letters from
southern coffee importers and other business leaders. At the
outset he announced that he wanted to be a citizen of Brazil.
He arrived with only one suit of clothes, but despite his thread-
bare aspect, he was welcomed by the minister of agriculture,
"more like a friend and equal than my shabby appearance would

seem to warrant me in expecting." At the minister's suggestion, Dunn looked to southern Brazil, down the Atlantic coast, for his Shangri-la.[9]

The book Dunn wrote about his scouting trip describes Brazil's climate as the finest and the healthiest "that is found in any country." It eulogizes Emperor Dom Pedro II, describes the commercial possibilities, and includes quotations from many other Confederates who had recently preceded him on the journey to Brazil.[10]

Dunn soon acquired a massive tract of land at Juquia in the state of São Paulo, choosing the name Lizzieland for it, in honor of his recently deceased wife, Elizabeth. Like areas of the western United States, it was a wilderness. It lay on the coastal lowlands, far from the nearest village, where the climate, though moderate, is somewhat warmer than the interior, which sits on a high plain.

Ready to move to his newly adopted country, Dunn returned to the United States to gather a group of emigrants. When the time arrived, several ships loaded with southerners left the ports of New Orleans, Baltimore, New York, Galveston, and Mobile, bound for Brazil. Most, like Dunn's group, planned to stop first in Rio, then take coastal steamers to their destination. Dunn's colony arrived aboard several ships, the largest being the *Marmion,* which had been chartered by the Brazilian government at a cost of forty thousand dollars. Yet each passenger was charged only sixty-two dollars, which could be paid over a period of four years. The ship left New Orleans on April 16, 1867, carrying over 350 refugees.

Almost all the passengers had once been wealthy, but now they had with them an average of only $216 each. Most of the men were from the Confederate army, including the two sons of William L. Yancey. There were cattlemen from Texas aboard and planters from the Mississippi Valley states as well.[11] One passenger, Julia L. Keyes, vividly described the journey in her diary.

The ship was stout, large and fast, but it had fallen on bad times in the postwar economic recession. It had been stripped bare by its previous owners and sailed without furniture. The travelers had to provide their own chairs, linens, and bedding. They also packed along canned fruits, wine, and crackers. The staterooms were improvised, some separated by curtains. The canvas hammocks were tiered three-deep.

The departure down the delta of the Mississippi River was on a beautiful spring morning. The vessel reached the Gulf of Mexico by evening, passed two ships stranded on a sandbar, and keeping an eye out for pirates—or wreckers, as they were called—headed southeast. Everyone was in high spirits, though they soon experienced seasickness and rough water. The ship bypassed St. Thomas because of an outbreak of cholera and yellow fever on that island.

Meals were served in large tin pans, one with boiled potatoes, another with bean soup, and the third, salted beef. Julia Keyes tells of a fight on board "between men of a low class."[12] Occasionally, in the evening the young people danced on deck to the music of an accordion.

Passing the mouth of the Amazon, fully sixty miles offshore, the emigrants noted that the ocean had turned a reddish color as the massive river's current pushed back the brine. One could dip a bucket and bring up fresh water.

On Thursday, May 16, they passed Cape Frio, fifty-six miles from Rio de Janeiro. At 8 P.M. they approached Raza lighthouse and the fort at the entrance of Rio harbor and dropped anchor, their 5,600-mile voyage complete. Such was the charm and beauty of Rio that American southerners were always to be captivated by it. No matter how many times one enters the harbor, the urge arises to somehow capture its essence in painting or song. Rio de Janeiro is a magnificent city in a lush tropical setting dotted with mountains that lead directly down to the Bay of Guanabara. Later, the Confederados confined to their isolated primitive surroundings, would harken back to their first few days spent in Brazil's capital city and wish that they could see it once again. A large percentage of them did return.

Julia Keyes describes her first view of the city:

> The dark clouds which had hung so drearily above us were breaking away. We had the glimpse of a rich sunset. Our prayers

were answered. We were permitted to behold this picture of wondrous beauty in its softest light. When in full view of Sugar-loaf mountain, the clouds rolled away and the full moon came out. . . . Rio in the light of morning presented another picture. We raised anchor and steamed up to the city at sunrise. . . . we saw the tiled-roof buildings again and the beautiful palm trees. . . . the Brazilians are fond of bright colors. Small, iron-railed balconies hang on the outside of the houses, in place of the graceful piazzas and verandas so necessary for comfort in [North] America. . . . once more on the ground . . . we walked up a broad road, covered with great white stones, making a curve on the mountain side . . . reached an immense iron gate and within were the grounds of our palace—the Government House in which we were to be sheltered.[13]

None of them, even those who had visited Europe, had ever seen such sights. The tropical gardens and palatial surroundings of the immigrants' hotel were unique.

At the time the Keyes family stayed in the Government House, they estimated the number of fellow guests at over three hundred. Others had already gone on to other parts of Brazil to begin their colonization. Two days after their arrival, the steamship *North America* came in from New York with another large number of immigrants. Later the emperor came to visit them. He was taken for a tour of the quarters where he inspected the food and conversed with the Confederates.

Rio's sophistication surprised most of the exiles. These southerners, many of whom had never been outside their own home states, delighted in the beautiful buildings, the lovely parks and botanical gardens. Some Brazilian customs astonished them, however. Eliza Kerr, one of the passengers on the *Marmion*, described one unusual practice. "I shall never forget," she wrote,

the first time our party saw a shower in rainy season. It began gently, gathered force quickly and in a few minutes rain was falling in sheets which converted the narrow streets into rushing torrents. Then, as suddenly, it decreased and stopped. The whole thing lasted less than an hour. The streets sloped from the stone sidewalks to the center, and in ten minutes after the rain ceased were beginning to dry. But while the rain poured and water covered the streets it was most amusing to see a procession of huge African negroes carrying elegantly dressed gentlemen across the streets. The gentlemen, wearing silk hats and carrying umbrellas, would stand bolt upright, holding themselves stiff, and the negroes would pick them up about the knees and wade the torrents, carrying them safe and dry to the other side.[14]

Rua de Direita, with its fine shade trees, broad flagstone sidewalks decorated with artistic patterns, benches, ice cream shops, restaurants, and stores, reminded the immigrants of Canal Street in New Orleans. They shopped at an English hardware store, went to the opera and the theater, sailed the bay, enjoying themselves even though they could not understand the Portuguese language.

Charles Nathan, an American who garnered a fortune building railroads for the emperor and had lived many years in Rio, frequently hosted the incoming Confederates at his beautiful home in the Botafogo section of the city. The American became kind of an advisor to the colonists, sometimes settling disputes, lending them money, and informing them of the rigors of living in the planned colonies.

Many of the Confederates went to Brazil without knowing which of the colonies they would join. The Freligh family, for example, had originally planned to join Colonel Gunter's group in its tropical setting three hundred miles north of Rio but had since been persuaded to go to the Reverend Dunn's settlement, five hundred miles south. The Gunter settlement could be reached on one of the two steamships the government temporarily provided. The Brazilians promised to establish permanent steamship lines to this and other settlements as soon as they became established.

THE VOYAGE OF THE MCMULLEN GROUP

Not all voyages were as untroubled as the *Marmion's*. Only seventeen people survived the sinking of the *Neptune* off the stormy coast of Cuba in the winter of 1866–67, and the passengers on the *Margaret* were all but wiped out by a smallpox epidemic on board. Nor was it easy to get clearance from port in a South that was under military occupation. It required persistence, fortitude, luck, and a few well-placed bribes. The going bribe rate for a shipload of colonists was $500.

The port of Galveston presented its own special problems. Earlier, Washington had sent General Sheridan down to Texas to prevent Confederates from crossing the Mexican border and setting up a government-in-exile. He had done his job so well that even the French army and its Foreign Legion, there to protect Maximilian, had pulled back from the border, fearful of causing an international incident. Sheridan's legacy remained in Galveston, a city of looted stores, as anarchic and burned-out-looking as any city in the South. There, a bureaucratic port authority was making passage out of Galveston harbor very difficult for Confederates seeking to leave, even though the hostilities had ended over a year earlier when the last Confederate warship had surrendered.

But Frank McMullen had done his job well. The leader of the expedition to New Texas in southern Brazil had chartered the *Derby* at minimum cost. The ship was of British registry, a twin-masted brig of 213 tons, with an oaken hull and square sails, which provided the sole, and economical, means of power. Unlike many oceangoing vessels of that time, the *Derby* did not possess even an auxiliary steam engine. In a good stiff wind, she could struggle along at six to eight knots. Though she looked a bit small to face the Atlantic's fury, the *Derby* was sturdy and wide.

McMullen had gathered one hundred forty-six Texans and eight Louisianians—plantation owners, their families, and their entourage—to make the journey. Among the group were McMullen's mother, two of his sisters, and a brother-in-law. By the standards of the time, the passengers were relatively prosperous. They had sufficient funds to charter a ship and outfit it for the voyage at a cost of fifteen thousand dollars. To modify it for emigration, the settlers had had additional bunks, partitions, and living accommodations constructed on the vessel, but even so, space and comfort were at a premium. The passageway between the living quarters was so narrow that only one person could move through at a time. A hole had been cut in the forward cabin to allow air to enter the below-decks sleeping quarters.

The cargo the settlers carried with them was valued at twenty-eight thousand dollars. They took along seeds, plows and other agricultural implements, wagons, and machinery. Several cotton gins and gristmills and metal-forging equipment added considerable weight to the cargo. They carried their firearms, cats, and hunting dogs, as well. To fit such extensive cargo and so many passengers into the ship had required careful planning. The *Derby*, which was twenty-eight feet wide and ninety-eight feet long, had only the interior space of a medium-sized house for cargo, crew, and 154 passengers.

The exile families carried only basic items for their journey—bedding, clothes, toiletries, tents, and precious family possessions such as wedding gowns, pictures, Bibles stuffed with papers showing births and deaths of family members, pressed flowers, and locks of hair. It was reported that these planters, before the war, were among the more prosperous, with net worths, on paper, of over a million dollars in current terms. They had been wiped out.

The voyage of the *Derby* was scheduled to begin on December 1, 1866, but by the third week in January there was still no sign of weighing anchor. The delay was irksome. All was not going well, despite the careful planning of the colony's organizer and leader Frank McMullen.

The passengers, most of whom had arrived weeks prior to the scheduled embarkation date, were quietly marking time but getting restless as excuses from the port authorities accumulated. They were told that the colony's papers were not in order, that their passports were not correctly issued, that special guarantees were needed, and that licenses had to be obtained. The immigrants believed that they were being deliberately harassed by the Yankee government and by the uncooperative ship's captain, as well. They spent their days lounging in their dockside tents, their eyes searching for indications that they would soon be underway.

Finally on the evening of January 24, Captain Cross,

McMullen and Colonel William Bowen called the voyagers together at dockside. My grandmother recollected what he said. "We're leaving on the morning tide, my friends," McMullen exulted, receiving in return a long cheer. "We have our papers in order and the dockmaster has just cleared us, thank God! Strike your tents and come aboard, all is ready."

The ship, no longer crammed against a dock, seemed to take on a new form as it cleared the harbor entrance two days later. Moving into the Gulf of Mexico, she strained forward with the wind, tearing a white furrow through the waves. In the dim early morning light, the lighthouse was almost the only landmark the ship's company could see. Once the *Derby* reached the deeper waters of the Gulf of Mexico, Captain Cross ordered the helmsman to make passage to the southeast, past Bolivar Peninsula and well out from the Louisiana and Mississippi coasts. The vessel picked up speed as the sails filled out, tightened, and heaved the ship forward.

Only the children had slept. Great Grandmother Thatcher stayed below with her four children. She had come along out of loyalty to her husband, but she had promised herself to return. "I'm coming back to Marshall, Texas, some day," she repeated to herself. Most Texans were on deck, some staring out, elbows resting on the rail. Jess Wright, ex-sheriff, still wore his six-shooters, looking a little out of place on a ship's deck.

Few of them would ever see their state again. It was a sadness beyond description that gripped them. Why had they left? Why not go to Mexico, just a few miles away, or to Cuba, where plantations still existed? Pardons could have been received merely for the asking. "Pardon for what? We haven't pardoned you Yankees yet."

At sea for seven days, the little *Derby* performed well in the headwinds she encountered. There was heavy weather all the way to the coast of Cuba, and the leaping waters battered the ship and sickened the passengers, but she pressed on.

On February 9 at Bahia Honda, on the northwest coast of Cuba a furious storm broke. Captain Cross headed for Havana harbor, skimming the shore. At four o'clock in the morning, the ship was pitched upward and came down with a crash on a rock; the craft heeled over on its side. All hands headed for the decks, crawling their way over spilled cargo and furniture. The dogs set up a howl. The night was pitch black, but the sandy shore was visible nearby.

The passengers and crew were told to hold on, though water was coming in through the side hatches. Then, an hour after it hit, the wind suddenly died, and the group found itself stranded well up on a beach. At dawn's light they climbed down and counted heads. All had survived. One crewman had a broken collarbone and was treated by Dr. George S. Barnsley, a colonist who was acting as ship's doctor. One half of the baggage was lost, and the remainder was so saturated with salt water as to be valueless. Only one gristmill was saved.

Cubans had begun to gather near the ship and some had started carrying away belongings that had floated away from the craft. As the colonists watched, one of the Cubans came up to the side of the ship, grabbed an armload of goods, and scampered away. Jess Wright leaned over the side and pumped three bullets into the man at a distance of sixty feet. The rest of crowd on the shore scattered at the crack of the gun.

Wright's hasty action was not well received by the Cuban authorities, and had it not been for the intercession of Confederates in Cuba, who had made friends with government officials there, Wright would probably have been marched against a firing squad wall.

A messenger was dispatched to Havana, and in a short time relief was sent. The ladies of Havana responded generously with clothing, food, and bedding. In Havana the Brazilian government arranged for them to be taken on the steamer *Mariposa* to New York to await another ship for Brazil. The *Mariposa* encountered yet another storm and put into Norfolk harbor for four days. From the deck the passengers could see Fortress Monroe, where Confederate President Jefferson Davis was being held in a cell. They cheered and yelled, but were too far away for Davis to hear them.

In New York City the southerners were welcomed by many ex-Confederates who had moved there, and the newspapers covered their arrival. The *New York Times,* in its March 28, 1867, issue reported the sad state of the shipwreck survivors.

> The steamer brought as passengers 150 emigrants who were on their way to Brazil, and who were wrecked off the coast of Cuba. These emigrants, who are now, through the kindness of General Goicuria of the Brazilian Emigration Agency of this city, quartered in the Collins' Hotel, consist of some sixty or sixty-five men and youths, the remainder being women and children and infants who appear to have suffered from the hardships they have undergone. Your reporter visited the party yesterday, and found them in a condition that must certainly excite the pity of all who see them. In one room were six women, some of them ladylike in appearance and manners, and eight or ten young children. Several of the women were dressed in clothes of fine texture, but now sadly worn and frayed—relics of more prosperous times. The men were with a few exceptions, hale and hearty looking and comfortably but coarsely clad. The majority of them had donned the Confederate gray, though a few appeared in good suits of broadcloth. Two or three of the men were sick with fever, and one tall youth—an unmistakable Southerner—appeared to be dying of consumption. As a general thing, however, they looked remarkably well in health for people who had undergone the perils and hardships of shipwreck and a protracted and stormy voyage.
>
> The majority of them are from Texas, a few coming from Louisiana. All are native Americans and appear to be possessed of rather more than average intelligence. They are principally agriculturists, a few being mechanics or machinists. It seems that about six months ago, finding affairs getting gradually worse in Texas, they commissioned Mr. Frank McMullen to proceed to Brazil and purchase on their account a tract of land suitable for the cultivation of cotton. He succeeded in procuring a fine piece of land at Sao Paulo.
>
> . . . Having missed the steamer of this month, the emigrants will be compelled to remain in their present rather uncomfortable quarters until the 22nd of April, when the Brazilian Emigration Agency will advance the funds necessary to enable them to reach their destination. In the meantime the women and children are suffering for the comforts, if not the necessities of life, and the charitably disposed will find a field for the exercise of their philanthropy. Contributions addressed to Mr. McMullen, at Collins' Hotel, Canal street, or the Brazilian Emigration Agency, No. 26½ Broadway will reach the persons for whom they are intended.

It is said that another large lot of emigrants from the South are expected here shortly, and that some 500 will soon sail from Mobile to settle at Para, on the Amazon—a location referred to by Prof. Agassiz as remarkably well adapted for the cultivation of cotton, sugar, spices, etc. The emigration agency expects that about 2,000 persons will leave this country during the Spring for Brazil.

Fresh from his scrape with Cuban law, "Cowboy" Jess Wright once again found cause to draw his guns. His hunting dogs were stolen from the hotel; so, strapping on his six-shooters, he stalked the thieves through the streets of the big city. His method was simple and direct, he whistled for the dogs as he tramped up and down the sidewalks. Finally, in front of a saloon he whistled again and immediately heard the two hounds begin to howl. The gray-clad westerner, like the fearless rebel troops at Gettysburg, pulled out both pistols and charged. He slammed through the swinging doors and pointed his guns, demanding his animals. He got them with little difficulty.

On April 22, on schedule, the survivors of the *Derby* embarked on the *North America* in company with a hundred of Dr. Gaston's colony, all of them heading for the Juquia area of Brazil. They arrived in Rio de Janeiro only two days after the *Marmion*, filling the magnificent emigrants' hotel. Their joy on arrival overflowed as they strolled among the rare flowers in the garden and experienced the long unaccustomed pleasures offered by the hotel. Great Grandmother Thatcher would long remember that "healing" month spent in the hotel.

COLONEL GUNTER'S COLONY

Most refugees from the South found that living in the Brazilian wilderness was still preferable to living under Yankee military occupation. Colonel Charles Gunter's group of southern lawyers, surgeons, and plantation owners was living under extremely primitive circumstances on the banks of Lake Juparana and the Rio Doce, in a lovely tropical setting on the malarial coast of central Brazil.

Probably nowhere in christendom had a more sophisticated, more thoroughly educated group ever voluntarily exiled itself into the wild, as this one had done. Two hundred souls cast their lot with the colonel. Colonists Josephine Foster, Julia Keyes, and Gunter have left in their writings a mass of evidence that this colony of American southerners had the wit and wisdom to understand what they were doing. They were not masochists, nor were they seeking martyrdom. They were simply in pursuit of a happy life.

Julia Keyes had cause to remember what Charles Nathan had said to her when she visited his palatial home in Rio de Janeiro before moving to Rio Doce. She wrote in her diary: "May 20, 1867—During dinner yesterday, Mr. Nathan made a remark which puzzled us, in reference to the Doce. He spoke of the wild life we would lead on the Doce, saying we would soon forget small forms of etiquette." Life would be hard for them in that primitive sector of Brazil where even Brazilians hesitated to settle, and the colonists knew it. In the same diary entry, Keyes wrote: "The Doce is mostly wild and uncultivated, and there is where we are going to live. Father is going to build us a home and then return to Rio to practice his profession [dentistry] and we will divide our time between the country and city."[15] The Keyes were intent on reestablishing the joyous days they and their eleven children had experienced in Montgomery, Alabama, before the war, when they had maintained both a city house and a plantation house.

Josephine Foster, previously of Chatawa, Pike County, Mississippi, had a double reason to be thankful for being on the River Doce. She had made the long trek across Texas into Mexico prior to the overthrow of Emperor Maximilian. There she had survived the bloody ouster of the Confederates attempting to set up colonies in the shadow of snowcapped volcanoes at Orizaba. From their homes on the beautiful lake and river, the colonists of Rio Doce could gaze into the distance and see the dark peaks of mountains among beautiful and everchanging surroundings, and the pioneering lady had only to imagine a snowcap on the mountaintops and be reminded of earlier, pleasant days at Orizaba.

States represented in the Gunter group were Louisiana, Texas, Florida, Alabama, Mississippi, and Virginia. Women who had never in their lives washed clothes or cooked food were pitching into manual labor with surprising vigor. Men whose work had been done by servants and laborers were digging ditches, hammering nails, and plowing fields behind balky Brazilian mules. Foster wrote:

> Lawyers, doctors, etc. have laid aside their professions, and have entered into their new life with the proper spirit, facing the forests, seemingly with the determination to succeed or die in the attempt. The ladies, too, are performing their part bravely, cooking, washing, etc. Such things seemed to come by chance in former years, but we thoroughly understand the process now. We act from a sense of duty, not pleasure, altogether. We already begin to reap the reward of our undertakings, in being happy and contented. We did not hope to enjoy such uninterrupted peace and quiet as we are now experiencing—each and all seem to be perfectly satisfied. We have had but little sickness among us, only slight chills, as all new settlers are subjected to in any country. We undergo hardships and privations, as a matter of course, but they are as nothing compared with what our forefathers underwent whilst settling Alabama, Mississippi, Louisiana and other states. [16]

Her fifty-seven-year-old father in less than a year had almost single-handedly cleared four acres of land and planted them with corn, beans, sweet potatoes, bananas, pineapples, grapes, ginger, and mandioca, "which is used by the natives as a substitute for corn, and we have already learned to love it, and there is nothing better for stock," wrote Josephine Foster. [17] The primitive house was comfortable, built to native specifications that allowed breezes to carry through the palm roof, an effective way of cooling the air. The dwelling had dirt floors, and much of the furniture was homemade. There was abundant meat in the woods and fish in the lake.

Some colonists were Catholics, but most were Protestants, many of whom keenly felt the lack of churches of their own faith. Many also resented restrictions imposed by the majority religion in Brazil, though the restrictions were few. One of these restrictions was that they were required to hold their services in buildings that were not built as churches. The colonies invited missionaries from the States to settle with them, and many responded, but Gunter's group was unable to attract a minister to Rio Doce.

From time to time one of the Confederates would complain about having to live in a country where there was "colored equality," but others would remind the objector that in the United States they would have to live with "negro superiority," referring to the many blacks who had been put into political office in the South by the dominant Republican party.

It may be true, as a Confederado descendant told Edwin McDowell of the *Wall Street Journal,* that southerners did not come to Brazil "with the thought of restoring the ante bellum South. Slavery was already on its way out here even before the American Civil War began. Importation of slaves was prohibited after 1850. I reckon maybe ten Confederates in these parts purchased Brazilian slaves, but that's all. American settlers weren't pro-slavery die-hards; many were just looking for better economic opportunities."[18] Most Confederados did not purchase slaves when they got to Brazil, and there is little evidence to show whether they would have done so had they had the money. Yet many Brazilian historians have written about the first-generation Confederados' racial prejudice, and many of the ex-Confederates living in Brazil in those days undoubtedly longed for the perpetuation of slavery.

First-generation Confederados had been raised to see slavery as the engine of economic progress in the South. Moral issues were sidetracked as cotton profits rose. Churches found enough ambiguous or even supporting passages in the Bible to convince themselves that slavery was permissible within Christian doctrine.

The color line the southerners had followed at home was disrupted by life in Brazil, where a person's class was far more important than his or her race. As one colonist remarked, in describing some of the group's wealthy Brazilian visitors, "Females could not visit a near neighbor without a servant in attendance and it was often difficult to tell which was the mistress—their complexions being the same. Among them were some negroes as black as Ethiopians."[19]

The abolitionist movement in Brazil was clearly winning

out when the southerners stepped off the ships. Perhaps some of the immigrants had begun to question the morality of slavery, although there is no written evidence to support this contention. Certainly, they were lured by the low cost of paid farm labor in Brazil, as well as by the possibility of owning slaves. Cotton was a labor-intensive crop. In a competitive world cotton market, cheap labor could provide a decisive edge over their compatriots who stayed in the U.S. In other words, many were impelled by reasons similar to those causing American corporations to move their production overseas in the latter part of the twentieth century.

Some Brazilian immigrants did buy slaves, of course. Although lacking capital in many cases, they knew how to raise it and to perpetuate large cotton-growing enterprises. Many bought their slaves as part of fully functioning *fazendas* (plantations). Captain Johnson of Florida, for example, bought his property near Rio with its thirty slaves and 95,000 coffee trees. Major McIntyre purchased a plantation at Ipaíba, and the sale included one hundred thirty slaves for the growing of coffee, sugarcane, and orange trees. One of the first acts of Colonel Norris when he came to Americana was to purchase three slaves. Another popular way of going into the agricultural business in Brazil was to rent the entire plantation. The Judkins family of Louisiana leased the Bangu Fazenda, together with its slaves. Among the Confederado families that owned slaves in the Americana colony were the Olivers, Halls, Harrises, Whitakers, Thatchers, Fergusons, Millers, Lands, and Coles.[20]

Slavery in Brazil was probably as cruel as it was in the U.S. But for the freed slave, especially if he were a mulatto, the two systems were markedly different. The freed slave in Brazil was the equal of any citizen there. His skin color, especially if he was as light-skinned as most American blacks, was not a handicap. His color did not necessarily bar him from active participation in all areas of Brazilian society. Being a mulatto meant that the person had some white blood in his veins, and so, he could move into the mainstream of the country's life. Many Confederados of the first generation never quite got used to the practice. To them, a man with *any* black blood was black, and

should stay in his own society. There was really little difference
between a freed slave and one still in bondage, they said. Even
the U.S. Supreme Court, until passage of the Fourteenth
Amendment to the Constitution, had held that race could
determine an American's citizenship rights. In the U.S. a freed
black was only partially free at that time.

Unlike the American free blacks, the freed slaves of Brazil
found real freedom when released from bondage. Moreover,
because there was no sharp color line, escape was easier, more
tempting, and more rewarding than it was in the U.S. Often a
slave simply walked away from a plantation. In the United
States, an escaped slave was easily distinguishable from the
whites around him. He had to dodge patrols that were con-
stantly on the lookout for runaways. But in Brazil, camouflage
was everywhere. Too many people of dark skin were walking
the streets, and a slave could get lost among them.

A few of the newly freed slaves in the United States emigrated side by side with the Confederates to Brazil. Best known
to the Americana colony was Auntie Silvy, who came with the
John Cole family and settled on their plantation near Santa
Barbara. She had been their house slave in the United States
and had chosen loyalty to the Cole family over exercising her
newfound freedom and staying in the U.S. Another ex-slave
who made the journey was a man named Rainey from South
Carolina, who was a riverboat pilot. He established a ferryboat
line between Rio de Janeiro and Niterói, on the other side of
Guanabara Bay.

Freedman Steve Watson was administrator of a São Paulo
sawmill, one of a string of enterprises owned by Judge Dyer of
Texas. Dyer had become the unofficial head of the New Texas
colony at the death of his nephew, Frank McMullen. Prior to
the Civil War Watson was Dyer's slave. Given his freedom at
war's end, he chose to remain with Dyer, whom he trusted,
rather than take his chances in a risky southern economy.

Watson, highly intelligent, was able to learn the Portuguese language, unlike most of the other colonists. He was an
able leader and helped build the sawmill into a profitable enterprise. Dyer's nephew, Columbus Watson, from whom the

freedman adopted his surname, was the third partner in the enterprises at New Texas. Products from the sawmill were transported by riverboat to Rio de Janeiro, finding a good market there. The enterprise came under severe financial strain, however, when their steamship was wrecked one stormy night at the entrance of the Juquia River. The loss was financially overwhelming and emotionally traumatic. Both Dyer and Columbus Watson soon succumbed to the homesickness that was permeating their deteriorating colony and headed back to the United States. Before leaving, however, they deeded all of the surviving property, the sawmill and twelve hundred acres of land, to Steve Watson, who they believed was adaptable enough to survive in that area.

Watson gathered the remains of the business, rebuilt it and became very wealthy, married a Brazilian lady, and raised a large family. He was highly admired in the region. In the area of the Juquia valley there are many Brazilian families with the name "Vassão," the Portuguese pronunciation of "Watson." His neighbors believed that, given a formal education, Watson would have been a *barão* (a baron); it was the highest compliment they could bestow on the American black who chose to cast his lot in southern Brazil.

Still, many first-generation Confederados had difficulty accepting blacks as their peers. So pronounced was their distaste that in 1888, when a senator opposed to slavery was assassinated on the eve of Brazil's emancipation, the Confederados were at first suspected. Nothing came of the investigation, but the suspicion itself is a sign of how different the former Confederates were from other Brazilians in this regard.

THE DEVELOPMENT OF SETTLEMENTS

Settlement at Rio Doce followed the pattern established at the McMullen colony (New Texas), the Dunn colony (Juquiá), and the Gaston colony (Xiririca), but these three were clustered together, while the Doce group was isolated five hundred miles to the north. All four groups intermixed to a small degree and kept in close communication. Events at one had repercussions in the other.

As might be expected, the first years were the hardest, and one of the worst hardships was the absence of steamboat transportation. The emperor had put comfortable steamships at their disposal on the initial leg of their trips from Rio to the colony sites. But the passengers and cargo were disembarked at the point where the river met the sea. In all cases, the colony sites selected were on shallow rivers, accessible only to canoes and, at flood tide, to paddle-wheel steamboats. The journey into the interior seemed designed to separate the wheat from the chaff.

The colonists and their supplies were taken from the steamships to shore in small boats. There they were compelled to wait a day or two for transport up the river, a distance averaging fifty miles. The wide canoes held both people and baggage with room to spare. Chairs were placed for the colonists to sit on. Some sat on boxes. White linen parasols were unfurled to counter the hot tropic sun, and the journey began.

Each canoe was powered by two men, who walked up and down the runways on either side of the craft, poling it along at a remarkable speed. The canoes moved smoothly through the water, except for an occasional bump into a sandbar. Gay conversation about their surroundings kept the passengers in good spirits. Mothers watched carefully over the children, especially those who showed signs of sickness.

At nightfall the boats were beached, and tents were erected. Meals were cooked over open fires, and sleep was obtained in defiance of the buzzing mosquitoes. Keyes described one close call:

> The mosquitoes were biting our baby boy and we could not fan them away. One of our little girls ran down to the canoes to get his long cloak that we might wrap up his feet. A frightened cry, in the next moment, reached our ears. . . . "Papa, Papa!" in so wild and mournful a tone! In attempting to reach the cloak from the outside canoe, while standing in the one nearest the shore, they separated and while holding on to the side of the boat, it pushed rapidly off, dragging the poor child down in the river. The water was twenty feet deep, at the banks, but she held firmly to the canoe until Father, hearing her cry, rushed down

and lifted her out. . . . What a beginning! What sinking of hearts.[21]

Not all mothers were lucky enough to rescue their children. Great Grandmother Thatcher had been against the voyage to Brazil from the very beginning, feeling in her bones that tragedy lay in store for her family. They had survived the wreck of the *Derby* on the Cuban shore and the dangers encountered during the voyage on the *Mariposa*. But at the mouth of the Juquía River, while helping load the canoes, her eldest son, Charles Emerson Thatcher, age eleven, missed his footing, plunged into the river, and was drowned before others could reach him in the swift waters.

The voyage up the river took about two days and two nights, the length of time depending on the river's current. The sun was so hot that the ladies covered the parasols with their shawls. They passed native huts on the riverbank and saw the Brazilians grinding sugarcane. They tasted sweet lemons and other exotic fruits growing along the water's course. Occasionally, the dusky oarsmen would sing. Toward evening the mosquitoes would begin to bite, but the colonists would be too tired to complain. Suddenly, the cry from the oarsmen "Linhares esta ahi!" would announce their arrival at the town of Linhares. There Colonel Gunter and his daughter Anna would be seen welcoming them from the riverbank.

Next day they would be up bright and early to meet the Confederates who were already established in the area, then they would be taken to their assigned temporary house, their residence for several weeks while they chose a plot of land on the shores of nearby Lake Juparana. An English blacksmith named Meagher acted as interpreter. He would go from house to house offering assistance. At times the young ladies and children, as well as some of the older colonists went down to the riverbank to wash their clothes on the stones, native style. They marveled at the cleanliness of the Brazilians. The native women wore a fresh, clean dress every day.

One day, while the men were off hunting for land, the ladies were frightened by the appearance of a large tribe of

58 *Noah's Ark*

Indians. The Indians were entirely naked with the exception of a knife strung around their necks. All was peaceful until in the evening the colonists began to hear howls and screeches as drunken Indians began dancing through the streets, but it turned out that this was a common ritual for the tribe and relatively harmless. The display was attributable to the supply of *cachasa*, the native rum, that the revelers had purchased earlier in the day and had sampled to an unhealthy degree.

The Indians in the southern part of Brazil were peaceful, but those colonists settling fifteen hundred miles north of the Doce colony had to be alert to their presence. One adventurous Confederate, after thoroughly learning the Portuguese language, wishing to know more about the friendly Brazilians, went traveling in the northern coastal state of Sergipe, looking for land to found a colony of his own. There he had the bad luck to be abducted by a hostile Indian tribe. According to Dr. Barnsley, one of the survivors of the *Derby*, the abducted man was a dentist, and had some medicines with him. On demonstrating his curative powers, he soon rose to the position of "medicine God" in the tribe and lived in privileged comfort among them for three years before escaping back to civilization. The experience cooled his ardor for Brazil. It was believed that he soon returned to his native Georgia to take his chances with the Yankees.

Just as the colonies south of Rio had a large number of Texans, the immigrants to the north, at the Rio Doce were frequently from Alabama. Regularly, the two sons of William L. Yancey, Captains Ben and Dalton, would drop around, and there would be reminiscences of the good old days in Montgomery. The social activities were similar to those held before in better times.

At the Rio Doce, Mrs. McDade had brought along, undamaged, a Wheeler & Wilson sewing machine, which she shared with the other ladies at regular sewing socials. Evenings were spent in the family dining room. For the benefit of company that dropped in, the family would display its photoengravings and a stereoscope. The Brazilians flocked to see the display, and this offered a way for the refugees to entertain them without having to exercise their woefully inadequate supply of Portuguese words. At times skillful Brazilian guitarists and singers would come by and entertain.

Finally the day would arrive when they could move to their own land. Again they would board native canoes, to be poled upriver, reaching their destination at Lake Juparana late in the evening. The Keyes's home was a palm-thatch hut, formerly a chicken roost, with a dirt floor and a fireplace.

When morning came, Lake Juparana was revealed as one of the loveliest places on earth, on a par with Lake Como, they thought. The beauty of nature made up for the barrenness of their living quarters. The Keyes found that they had physicians as neighbors on both sides, one from Alabama and the other from Virginia. Nearby, also, were Dr. Farley and the Cogburns from Alabama. Other physicians, including Dr. Dunn and Dr. Berney were in the neighborhood. Mail from the States was delivered every two weeks.

The immigrants busily added to their huts, making them into comfortable houses, and whitewashed them neatly. The houses were built native style. Poles were first driven into the ground and then roof poles were tied to them with a strong vine. No nails were used. After this framework was tied to-gether, daubing with clay created the walls, and a roof of palm leaves was applied. The building of a house was an event in which the whole neighborhood participated. Americans and natives alike pitched in to daub. The floor was made of layers of clay, each of which was pounded with heavy wooden pestles, making it as hard as rock. Later, all of the Americans were able to put in wood floors when Dr. Farley established a sawmill.

At times the Confederados attempted to improve on the Brazilian way of building houses. Some insisted on putting American-style shingles on the roof, instead of the palm leaves. To their consternation the heavy tropical rain easily penetrated the shingles, and they had to be replaced with palms.

Life in the wild had its compensations. Every morning the settlers would walk directly from their beds down to the white, sandy beach in front of their houses and bathe in the warm waters of the lake. A little nook was found in the bushes for dressing. No discomfort was felt in such a mild climate, uniform throughout the year. The colonists enjoyed the absence of flies, a constant annoyance back home in the U.S.A. Brazilian mosquitoes, however, seemed to be even less friendly than the U.S. variety. The lake was not only a thing of beauty and recreation, it was the road by which they visited each other and brought in supplies. Jennie Keyes, Julia's daughter, enjoyed watching the canoes go by with their white sails glimmering in the sun. The Americans had introduced sails to the canoes, and the Brazilians were copying the fashion.

The Millers, before they moved south to Americana, were prominent members of the Gunter colony, and they entertained widely. Christmas at their house that first year was a grand occasion, with a huge baked turkey crowning the dinner table. In only nine months, they had transformed their home at lakeside into a showpiece. Thoughts of those present around the well-stocked table were about their loved ones back in Mississippi, Alabama, Georgia, and the other states of the old Confederacy, struggling to survive. They missed their friends and relatives back in America. Separation had formed a permanent ache that not even a physician could cure. Some wondered whether their grandparents and great grandparents had felt the same ache when settling the wilderness in the South.

Colonel Gunter, who had gotten several months' start on the other settlers had the finest crop the first year. Though plagued with the malarial fevers, as were many of the colonists, his family worked hard in the fields and grew fine watermelons and sweet potatoes, which they divided with the neighbors.

The Rio Doce settlement went through a series of misfortunes beginning in 1868. Many of the settlers were stricken with malaria, a virulent form not unlike the malaria prevalent at the time in the southern coastal areas of the United States. Quinine supplies sometimes were limited and real suffering occurred, though there were no fatalities. A drought, the worst in thirty years, ruined many of the crops. The Keyes family decided to move to Rio and left their plantation with the Spencers. Others moved to other colonies or set up independent plantations of their own.

The colony never grew from its original size, yet it prospered in the long run. Planters came and went, some acquired riches, others barely survived. The vast number of professional men in the colony in time sought their fortunes in the larger cities of Brazil, particularly Rio, where life was even grander than they had experienced in the U.S. South. In Rio one could sample the best of Europe. Women wore Parisian fashions, the best people drank only French wines, traveled in liveried carriages, lived in palatial houses made not of daubed clay but of exquisitely cut marble and brick. Long winding driveways led to the front door. There was a great demand for physicians, and most established large practices. The first of them to move, Dr. McDade, settled at Itapemirim. In his first year he had many patients.

The sacrifices of living in the country paid dividends later to some of the children of the refugees, as in the case of the leader of the Rio Doce group, Colonel Gunter. Along with many of the original settlers on the Rio Doce, Colonel Gunter stayed on the land and continued to develop his cotton, coffee, and sugarcane fields. He died there on August 19, 1873, seven years after his arrival, leaving quite a legacy. His son, Basil Manley Gunter, was named a consular representative of the United States government in Victoria in 1889, though he was a Brazilian citizen. He invested heavily in the Brazilian Railway System and amassed a fortune, living his entire life in Brazil.

Despite the permanence of the settlement, the government of Brazil was never able to establish a regular steamship line to the colony site at Lake Juparana. For this reason, the Confederados found it difficult and expensive, though not impossible, to transport their products to other parts of the country. Some, therefore, moved away in the 1880s, among them the Bunnells of Alabama and the Brassell family of Georgia, who returned to Mexico.

New Texas, Xiririca, and Juquía, in the southern, cooler part of Brazil could claim similar failures and successes. New Texas was demoralized by the death of its leader Frank McMullen. This honest and talented man had made the trip while in the painful throes of tuberculosis. He did not slacken his pace or get proper rest in directing his colonists to their places on the banks of the Juquía River.

As had happened at the Rio Doce, the vast plots of land given to these three adjoining colonies did not receive enough settlers to warrant the establishment of a regular paddle-wheel riverboat line. When it became apparent that the government was not able to do it, some settlers tried to set up a private line. But the boats went aground on the rocks at the river's entrance, where they were forced to navigate across shifting sandbars on unchartered, undredged streams. It was a vicious circle that put a slow economic squeeze on the settlers as word of the success of the Americana–Santa Barbara plantations reached them.

The Reverend Dunn, whose intentions are still wrapped in mystery, took leave of his flock three months after arriving at his Lizzieland. Some Confederados to this day believe that the parson absconded with funds belonging to some of the colonists. The Miller family, in particular, was understood to have taken an oath that "that was the last preacher we would ever lend money to." Dunn was the only leader whose motives were ever questioned, but the evidence against him was circumstantial. As soon as his group reached Brazil, letters were received by the southern press, warning prospective emigrants against "this swindler."[22]

In his wake, Dunn left four hundred Americans scattered across a plot of land as large as the state of Delaware, and over time, they blended into the Brazilian surroundings. It is reported by a traveler to the Dunn colony in 1896 that only six houses were still being occupied by the Confederado families. The site was overgrown with vegetation, and even the road was covered with weeds. There was no post office, no church, and the steamboats had stopped coming up the river.[23]

On paper the economics of the colonization schemes seemed foolproof. Everything—from special dispensation from the government and transportation to housing, roads, lumber, gristmills, and even nails—had been attended to. But one by one the settlements split apart, and the people moved to other areas of Brazil. Somehow, isolation in Brazil was not as bearable as isolation in the United States. Many of the dedicated agriculturists found excellent land in São Paulo's interior, but the bulk of the colonists went to the cities of São Paulo and Rio de Janeiro. The Miller family of the Rio Doce moved to Americana because of the coffee-growing boom. Since there were now two Miller families in Americana, these were called the Doce (the Portuguese word for sweet) Millers, and the others were teasingly referred to as the amargo (sour) Millers.

The westward frontier migration pattern of the agricultural Americans across North America was different in important ways from the Brazilian pioneering of southerners. The western pioneers usually tried to settle around a village that provided essential services. The services were not preplanned, but like the proverbial "invisible hand" of Adam Smith, they appeared, many in response to letters from settlers already at the location—as in this letter from a settler in the West. "We have," he wrote, "a store, a church, a hotel and a schoolhouse. The store has a big stock of goods, from garden seed to silk dresses; the hotel is a good one, with everything to attract the drummer or the tourist; the school is the best for miles around, and our church is the pride of the place. What we want now is a paper."[24]

In the West, many of the hardships were the same as in Brazil: enforced isolation, poor roads, and unpredictable river transportation. Brazil's colonists faced a longer voyage to their destination, but they were not beset by hostile Indians or menaced by the brutal western winters.

Almost all of the Confederate colonies however, copied the pattern of the Dunn settlement. All possessed an over-abundance of good lands and fine forests. But in an attempt to adhere to the southern plantation way of life, they built their homes far from each other on oversized plots of farm and woodland averaging twelve hundred acres. There was no provision for a central town. The Confederados tried to re-create the large, successful riverfront plantations of the South. They aimed to be self-sufficient, independent of as many outside supporting services as possible. Even in the U.S. South, however, only a few massive plantations could claim almost total self-sufficiency. Southerners who settled in Brazil thus found themselves too scattered to generate the trading activity needed to support a town and, as a result, often deprived of many things they might otherwise have had.

Americana did not follow this pattern. It arose because Confederados staked out their properties as close to the coming rail lines as possible. This cluster of houses represented the beginning of a town. Then, with good transportation available, Americana just grew.

One of the most highly respected colonizers was Dr. James Gaston. His colony at the headwaters of the Ribeira River, eight days' journey from the mouth at Iguape, upstream from McMullen's and Dunn's, consisted of about a hundred persons, mainly from the Carolinas. They faced the same trials as the other Confederados endured, and some made their choice to move to other areas of Brazil. Gaston himself moved several times, finally setting up his medical practice in the city of Campinas, not far from Americana. By 1871 the colony had spread itself so thin through dispersal of its residents that they were hard to trace. Most settled in other parts of Brazil. One of the exceptions was William, the Redhead, who married one of the neighboring Brazilian girls, absorbing the native culture entirely. His descendants who populate the area, sometimes can be spotted by their red hair and blue eyes.[25]

The next state south of São Paulo is Paraná, site of the southernmost colony of Confederates. Immigrants to this state, which lies near the frost line, had to take along their woolen clothing and build fireplaces in their homes. The chosen location rivaled Rio de Janeiro in beauty, and excelled it with its less humid climate. It was separated from the Lizzieland and New Texas colonies to the north by over a hundred miles. The lands for the settlement were selected by Colonel M. S. McSwain and Horace Lane of Louisiana. Many of the settlers were from Missouri, among them Issac Young, Dr. John H. Blue, Judge John Guillet, and the Budd, Johnson, Young, Patterson, Parker, Fife, Comb, Glenn, and Thompson families.

> Dr. Blue, in addition to operating a plantation, practiced medicine in the town of Paranagua. Isaac Young purchased 8,000 acres of land, 5,000 of which were covered with fine

timber, and 150 in cultivation, for the sum of $5,600, and with the land improvement worth double the price. On the tillable portion of the plantation he proceeded to the exploitation of negro [slave] labor in the production of cane, corn, beans, potatoes, mandioca, and other products. Through the use of water power he operated the cane and mandioca mills and the two distilleries that came with the place. Little wonder that he could pity the folks back in Missouri, where the "radicals" were in the hey-day of their power; and "would not exchange my situation, with my lands and woods and water power, for the Gubernatorial Chair in Jefferson City, nor even be a "military governor" of two southern states [then under military occupation]. The only great disadvantage that seemed to circumscribe his happiness was "ignorance of the Portuguese language."[26]

To their credit, Dr. Blue and Isaac Young learned to speak Portuguese within three years. Others did equally well in beautiful Paranagua. James K. Miller owned a barrel-making enterprise. Dr. M. S. Fife, Isaac Young, and W. P. Budd organized the Paraná Manufacturing Company, which was immediately successful. The several hundred members of the Paraná colony were difficult to trace since most of the members lived far apart from each other. Some returned to the United States, others blended with the other ethnic groups in the area, most notably the Germans and are almost lost from sight.

Some southerners could not adapt, and the U.S. minister tried to persuade Washington to help, but the United States held off from assisting the Confederates who wanted to return but lacked the means. The minister wanted the U.S. government to contract with the Brazil Steamship Line for a large vessel. However, the most Washington would do was permit U.S. navy vessels to pick up a few returnees each year. The cruiser *Kansas* took back eleven in 1869, the *Quinnebaug* returned thirty in 1870, and twenty-four came back aboard the *Portsmouth* in 1871. The sixty-five returnees were well publicized in the U.S. press of the time, and almost all the stories were slanted to give the impression of a mass return of the Confederates from Brazil. Meanwhile ships loaded with southerners continued to leave the ports of Baltimore, Mobile, New Orleans, New York, and Galveston for ports in Brazil.

TEXAS FEVER AND DEPLETED LANDS

By 1870 the dreams of the colony leaders McMullen, Dunn, Gunter, and Gaston of a Brazilian Valhalla were already dying. No mass migration from the United States on the scale envisioned by these men occurred. The groups of immigrants who did come had begun to spread out and to lose their identity as restless families moved away from their original plots of land. Already, signs of Brazilianization were appearing as they began to use and understand the Portuguese language, and native cultural influences began to erode and separate the fabric of their communities.

These warriors loose in Brazil were not adept at the confinements of group living. Some have said that Confederates were the world's most intense individualists since the Italian Renaissance and its men of "terrible fury." This quality served them well in battle against numerically superior Union forces, but was ill suited to colonizing. Moreover, they had settled in areas unsuited to the growing of cotton and coffee, the mass bonanza crops that were naturally of most interest to men accustomed to thinking on a grand scale.

The combined economic and psychological factors doomed the communities to early extinction. Soon dispersed were New Texas, Paranagua, the Amazon group, Iguape, and Rio Doce. Only Santa Barbara (later called Americana) was still growing in the 1870s. It would succeed because its *terra roxa* (red clay soil) offered, for a while, great riches to the planters. Following the hazy, inexorable laws of economics, São Paulo state attracted Confederados from all parts of Brazil. Americana lay on the path of the westward-moving search for productive, new soil that the farmers would deplete before moving on.

An American agricultural expert, who traveled through São Paulo state in the twentieth century, wrote:

> The history of the countryside was not much different from that of our own cotton South. Poor agricultural methods and exploitation without intelligence had gradually ruined the land over generations and even centuries. The freeing of slave labor was given as the excuse for the final decline and ruin but it was no

more a genuine reason and it had no more validity than the same
excuse in relation to the dying agricultural economy of our own
South. Both areas would have gone down into ruin if the slave
labor had never been set free. Both areas were ruined by their
own proprietors.[27]

This pattern of deplete-and-move, deplete-and-move persisted,
resulting in forced migration for many of the families and
further fragmentation of Confederate communities.

Many were seeking their fortunes like their adventurous
fathers before them, who had moved relentlessly from southern
Virginia, across Alabama, Mississippi, and finally into Texas—
"Texas fever" newspapers called the movement—in the search
for new cotton land to replace worn-out fields. The trail in
Brazil was similarly well-trodden, and westward as well.

All the talk in Brazil when the colonists arrived was about
coffee. None of the southerners had ever seen a coffee tree
before, but they quickly learned of the potential riches awaiting
the successful planter of the tiny beans, and eventually they
would turn to growing it. It was like mining gold, but with far
better odds of striking it rich.

The Brazilians had imported the coffee trees from French
Guiana in the early eighteenth century, planting them in the
Paraíba valley northwest of Rio de Janeiro. As the thirst for the
brew increased around the world, coffee growing spread into
São Paulo, Minas Gerais, Paraná—states to the south and west
of Rio de Janeiro—moving eventually across the border into
Uruguay in the twentieth century. The boom reached its peak
in the 1860s and the immense fortunes made during that time
were manifested in the beautiful mansions in downtown Rio
and São Paulo. Many of these ornate structures still house these
"old money" families.

Almost instinctively the Confederados supplanted the
familiar Texas fever with São Paulo fever. They began by planting the familiar cotton, for which the Santa Barbara area was
ideal. There was adequate rainfall, no fear of frost, and fertile,
virgin soil. The farmers made little effort to retain the fertility
of the soil, dooming the plantations to extinction after ten or
twelve years of high yield. But meanwhile, they were making

sizable profits. When the land gave out, the farmers moved. Grandfather Harris became so accustomed to the frequent moves that he refused to buy a house. Even after he retired, he remained secure in the belief that soon he would be moving again.

The southerners may have depleted some of Brazil's lands, but they also contributed to the country's development by showing their neighbors the advantages of the plow over the hoe. This improvement in farming methods produced increases in crop yields in many parts of Brazil. In addition, the southerners manufactured plows for sale in Brazil, helping to expand their use. Niels Nielsen, whose migrating instincts had taken him from a village in Sweden to join the Confederate cause in Alabama, headed the successful Fabrica de Arados (plow factory) in Santa Barbara.

Brazilians noted that the incoming Americana group was blessed with some of the U.S. South's better agricultural specialists, and they hired them as advisors. Many were also employed as administrators of the big plantations. Grandfather Harris got his start this way. Trading on their know-how, these southerners then acquired their own land on good credit terms.

The southérners tried to set up their plantations quickly, for there was little to gain from wasting time and living off their savings. Most had always left the details of their agricultural activities to their overseers and agents when they had lived back in the cotton South. Now, they found themselves on their own, forced to master the minute aspects of Brazilian commerce and economics and to learn how to grow the unfamiliar coffee and sugarcane. In most cases their mercantile instincts prevailed, however, and they prospered.

The Halls, Thatchers, Gastons, and other Confederado families profited heavily from their first cotton planting. Some claimed to have netted a 100 percent return on their investment within two years. Thus, for many of those who came to São Paulo, the dream of transplanting their southern life to another country, had finally come true. The Old South mansions began to be built once again.

AMERICANA'S BEGINNINGS

The Santa Barbara colony began with Colonel William H. Norris, who purchased a five-hundred-acre tract on the undeveloped Machadinho Estate near Santa Barbara. Beginning cautiously, he bought three slaves, two for the fields and one to help with the housework. The soil, climate, and topography was identical to that of his own Perry County in southern Alabama.

Colonel Norris had been an Alabama state senator and political ally of the firebrand orator of the Confederacy William Lowndes Yancey. He fought in the Mexican War but was too old to serve with Confederate forces. As one of his descendants remembered "Colonel Norris was 65 when he came to Brazil. He didn't know anything about Brazil or the language. But he was mad enough to want to try to make a go of it."[28]

Norris had brought gold with him to Brazil—estimates ran as high as a hundred thousand dollars' worth, 1984 value—which was said to have escaped the hands of General Sherman's marauding soldiers. The story told was that a Union officer recognized the colonel as a fellow Freemason when Norris's wife gave him the secret hand sign. The Union officer then stopped the soldiers who were digging up the horde in Norris's front yard. Family members have denied that Colonel Norris had as much money as rumored when he came to Brazil. However, in 1866, almost a year after General Robert E. Lee had surrendered at Appomattox Courthouse, Norris wrote his son Frank, who had chosen to stay in Alabama, that his first year in Brazil was a financial success. He had netted the equivalent of fifty thousand dollars, some of it gained through the colonel's efforts as an agricultural consultant.

First-generation Confederates like Colonel Norris continued to consider themselves Americans. They were from the C.S.A. not the U.S.A.; but still they were Americans, linked firmly to George Washington, Thomas Jefferson, James Madison, and the colonial heritage. The Fourth of July holiday was the major event of the year. Therefore, it should come as no surprise that the name of their town became Americana. But it was the Brazilians in the neighborhood who chose that name, in reference to the place where their neighbors, the Americanos, lived.

In the 1870s, when the railroad from São Paulo was completed, the Confederados had begun to build their houses near the railroad station, several miles east of Santa Barbara. For approximately twenty-five years the cluster of homes and shops grew and the settlement took on the name Estação (the station). The Brazilians, however, always called the town Villa Americana in response to the obviously foreign ethnic character of its majority population.

Province authorities, recognizing the need to offer proper fire, police, and sanitary services to the group around the station met in January 1900 and incorporated the town, arbitrarily naming it Americana. The Confederados offered no objection to the choice. They themselves, though, continued to call it the station long into the twentieth century.

The logotype of the Confederate descendants' organization symbolizes the joining of two cultures—the Brazilian and the American.

FOUR

America City, Brazil

The state of Sao Paulo is Brazil's most important industrial and agricultural unit, and its output is reportedly equal to that of the remaining twenty Brazilian states! . . . More cotton is produced and marketed in this district than in all the Latin American nations combined.
.U.S. Navy Midshipman's Cruise Guide

C ERTAIN Amazon Indian tribes decorate their pottery with the design of the Confederate flag, the result of having encountered the colonists who chose to settle in that vast jungle. There have been other, more profound effects of the migration, though perhaps none more dramatic. All the Joneses, Thatchers, Harrises, Bufords, Coachmans, and Yanceys that swooped down on Brazil gave something to the country they had chosen and took something from it. They were hospitable people who came to a hospitable country. In the words of a writer who visited the Confederados in 1974, "Brazil is a land of people who are kind and warm, and have not yet let modern pressures erase the niceties of yesteryear. But even they are impressed with the folks in Americana and their southern hospitality. 'Ah, Americana! Very good people, very Christian,' pronounced a Brazilian expansively at the mention of the city's name. 'It is always come eat at my house, come eat at my house!'"[1]

There have been no in-depth studies by U.S. social scientists to test the qualities and the impact of the American

71

character when reimplanted overseas. Brazilians, though, have taken up some of the slack. Some of their observers have measured the impact of those few thousand North Americans. José Artur Rios, for example, said of the Confederados: "Something of their spirit passed into the local life. They enriched our society with their progressive mind, their capacity for action, and their technical competence, and perhaps in the hearts of their São Paulo descendants has filtered a little of that love of freedom, an American tradition, and that pride of the old planter that is a Southern tradition."[2] Others frequently noted the energy displayed by the Confederates, who not only were able to establish meaningful lives for themselves in Brazil but also founded schools, churches, hospitals, businesses, and factories in all parts of that country. One commented that the American expression "time is money" had transformed Brazilians of the middle and upper classes into champions of efficiency and speed.[3] Descendant Pamela Ann Huber recalls that many Brazilians considered the emigrants the nineteenth-century equivalent of workaholics. "If you shut one of them up in a room without work to do he would go crazy," they would remark.

In the twentieth century a large number of the Confederados went into the professions after moving away from the plantations of their fathers. Many of them were physicians. Dr. Franklin Pyles became one of the country's leading surgeons. Dentistry, however, seemed to benefit most by the influx of professionally trained Confederates. In the United States, it was once widely believed that the only good psychiatrists were those with Viennese accents. Similarly, many Brazilians came to believe that a dentist almost had to be an American to be effective. Margaret Meade's colleague, Gilberto Freyre, who had studied the effect of Americans on the transportation system, agriculture, education, and medicine in Brazil, wrote: "The American dentist became an institution. Even an Englishman like Dr. Rawlinson of Recife, styled himself an 'American' dentist."[4]

One of the more colorful and successful dentists was Dr.

John W. Coachman, who in the 1920s would recount his adventures in the Confederate navy, sometimes punctuating the story by marching around the room holding his umbrella to his shoulder and whistling "Dixie." His granddaughter, Alice Coachman Ferro, tells a story about Coachman's pioneering days. While he was moving his family from one location to another, the boat they were traveling in struck an underwater log and capsized. The family—father, mother, and six children and another Confederado, Ruland Freligh—were saved by holding onto the log until help arrived. Later, Dr. Coachman had a piece of the log cut off and inscribed to commemorate that eventful day.

Like most other settlers, the Coachmans scattered across the face of Brazil. They started in Rio de Janeiro, moved to the state of São Paulo, four hundred miles to the southwest, living mainly in the city of São Paulo itself. Their Confederado friends and relatives were within a 150-mile radius in places with names like Piracicaba; Bauru, home of the large Smith family; Jaú; Campinas; and Santa Barbara.

The Coachmans blazed the trail of dentistry across that part of the country, establishing something of a dynasty in the process. Today one still finds three Coachmans practicing in the metropolis of São Paulo: Drs. Charles S. Coachman, Robert G. Coachman, and Carlos Escobar Coachman.

In 1911 Hentz Coachman was the Brazil agent for the White Motor Company. The U.S. company, very successful in the early days of the automobile, featured a steam-powered auto that Coachman would drive through the bustling city, catching the interest of the passersby. "Onde e o cavalo?" (Where's the horse?) they would holler.

The Confederados have had their impact on Brazilian music. Some of the country's most talented musicians are descendants. Until her death in the 1940s, Elsie Houston, great grandniece of the immortal Texan, Sam Houston, was one of Brazil's most popular singers. She and my mother were very close friends, and Elsie used to delight in taking us, the children, off Mother's hands. On occasion, the four of us, Elsie, my sister Lucia, brother John, and I, would set off on a tour of fashionable Avenida Rio Branco's marvelous ice cream and custard shops.

The name Lee still lives in Brazil through music. In 1984 Rita Lee was named Brazil's most popular singer of the year. She has been acclaimed for her native Brazilian interpretations in the international world of pop music. She is the daughter of Charles Fenley Jones, who honored the memory of the commander of the Army of Northern Virginia in all his daughters' names; Rita's sisters are Mary Lee and Virginia Lee Jones. Rita Lee, who dropped the Jones for professional reasons, began her singing career with a São Paulo rock group in the 1960s. She has risen steadily to stardom, making many records, which are also popular in the United States and in the Spanish-speaking countries. Her uncle, Leonard Yancey Jones was the founder of public radio in São Paulo.

One of the radio commentators most familiar to many Brazilians is Mary Miller, who reports from New York City for the Voice of America. She is the granddaughter of Mary Thompson Norris of Americana. Mary Miller came to the U.S. in 1960 to study at New York University. While there, she began broadcasting a Portuguese-language program over station WRUL. Her pleasing voice and faultless Portuguese gained her a job with the Voice of America.

Among the many Confederado descendants is Charity Crocker Cole, wife of Dennis Cole, headmaster of the British school located in Niterói, a suburb of Rio. Many other Confederados have close links to the British community in Brazil. The ties have their origin in the Civil War era when the British unofficially supported the South in her struggle. Our own family, for example, belonged to the Church of England in Rio. My brother, John, and I were active participants in a British Boy Scout troop. We always looked forward to Empire Day when, together with many of the Confederados, we celebrated the British holiday at the Cricket Club in Niterói, marching with them and joining in their games and hip-hip-hurrahs. As children we felt doubly blessed to enjoy both the British celebration and our own boisterous Fourth of July festivities at the American Club on Visconde de Pirajá Street in Ipanema. We always invited the British to join us.

Mother liked to note the contrast between her old church in the state of São Paulo and the ornate, very formal British church in Rio. She remembered the rough, unpainted pews of the countryside Old South Methodist Church in Americana where the preachers would declare that the "Second Coming will be when Catholic Brazil becomes totally Protestant." "Preachin' Sundays" at the rural Confederado community were the high point of the week, culminating occasionally in an impromptu service for the prisoners in the local jail, for which members of the congregation would carry along the portable pump organ.

For rest and relaxation, the Confederados of Rio went to the island of Paquetá, a two-hour ferryboat ride from downtown Rio. The tropical paradise, with its lovely homes and gracious seaside restaurants, was a favorite of the emperor and still remains popular with Brazilians today.

In 1935 we were visited in Rio by the U.S. navy cruiser *Tuscaloosa*, on its maiden voyage to the South Atlantic. The ship, named after the Alabama city, was a focus of our attention during its two-week stay. The officers invited us aboard for a visit. Escorted by Warrant Officer Forrest P. Brown, we dined with the sailors, eating "real" American food, some of it— including tomato soup and ham sweetened with syrup and pineapple—totally foreign to us. After dinner we all went on deck for a showing of the new Hollywood movie *The Bat*. Later in the week we hosted the officers at a dinner at our house.

One reason that Confederados are hard to spot in Brazil is that many of them changed their names down through the years. Like immigrants to the United States, the Confederados often discovered that their names were difficult for the locals to pronounce. Warren Hoge, in an August 19, 1979, *New York Times* story, reported that Confederates frequently changed their names to accommodate to the new land. The McFadden family, for example, altered the spelling of their name to Mac-Fadden "to make the name intelligible to Brazilians." The American arriving with an unpronounceable name, found him-

self at a disadvantage in the new society. MacKnight, for example, would be pronounced Mahg-nee-git or Mahg-neech-tay.
Harris became Ah-reece; Jones came out Jaw-ness; Whitaker
was pronounced Ooee-tah-cray. Inevitably, Confederate names
came to be spelled as they were pronounced, and Watson,
became Vassão, for example.

Among the American imports to Brazil was MacKenzie
University of São Paulo, which was founded by American missionaries drawn there by the Confederados. The university is
recognized as one of the best in Latin America, especially in its
School of Engineering. There are dozens of American/
Confederado schools in Brazil, which have helped shape the
country's educational system. I was exposed to a stern Confederado education at the Bennett School in Rio de Janeiro.
The school, affiliated with the Methodist church, was founded
by Confederados. My mother taught in several Confederado
schools, to which it became fashionable for Brazilians to send
their children.

Many of Brazil's railroads and vast public works projects
were constructed by companies owned or managed by Confederados. One of the most ambitious ventures was the leveling
of a mountain in the middle of Rio de Janeiro. The rock was
pushed into the harbor to form additional waterfront land.
Uncle Simeon Harris was engineer on the 1913 project, and his
assistant was Kermit Roosevelt, son of President Theodore
Roosevelt. Kermit's presence in Brazil was a contributing factor
to Roosevelt's decision to come down and explore the Amazon
that year. Uncle Sim and Kermit became good friends and, on
occasion, swapped Civil War horror stories. Kermit's grandmother's plantation in Roswell, Georgia, had survived the war
despite its location in the path of Sherman's forces.

Uncle Simeon later became a partner in the international
law firm Momsen and Harris, which later operated in Brazil
under the name Momsen and Leonardo, following his death in
1943. Uncle Gib Harris was a plantation manager and also
served as an official with the American embassy. His son, John
Wesley Harris, is professor of mathematics at Rio de Janeiro's
Federal University. Noelina, John's wife, is also a university

professor. My first cousin, Pulu Harris Domschke is a talented artist in the Rio de Janeiro area. Another is Elizabeth Harris Cannone, whose comely features won her the title of Miss Leblon in the finals of the Miss Brazil beauty contest. Confederados were often employed by U.S. banks and industrial firms with offices in Brazil. There are over thirty-five hundred American branches in the city of São Paulo alone. Among the most successful industries in Brazil are the home-owned soft drink bottling plants. Horace Pyles formed a company called Crush, that produces a tasty orange drink popular in Brazil.

When I lived in Brazil all Americans were assumed to be rich or, at the very least, highly respected in their profession. It felt as though the English language was the key to success. It seemed to me then that Americans simply never worked with their hands, and it seemed that way to others also. Once in 1935 we called for a plumber to fix a leaky pipe. The man who showed up at our door was an American. The sight of someone from our ancestor country, speaking English, carrying tools, and working with his hands was unsettling. The whole family crowded around to take a look at this strange Martian creature. He turned out to be a recent arrival who had jumped ship at the port of Rio, a victim, he told us, of something called an economic depression in the U.S.

The Confederado community still lived its patrician, Old South way. At the Hervey Hall Plantation it was as though prewar Savannah, Charleston, and Vicksburg had parachuted down among the banana and mango trees. Scarlett O'Hara would have found a comfortable home there, and indeed, readers of Margaret Mitchell's *Gone with the Wind* have noted that the idea of Scarlett's fleeing to Latin America was mentioned twice in its pages. Grandfather and the colonists took their cultural baggage with them on their sailing ships of the 1860s. Even unto the third generation it was easy to note the romanticism, the dignity, the fanatic family cohesion, the love of heroics, and the sentimental snobbishness.

In commerce, it was necessary to speak Portuguese, but at home the Confederados spoke English exclusively, sometimes into the third generation. Today, most speak Portuguese at home but use their English at every opportunity. Robert E. Lee Conti, a young fifth-generation descendant speaks English almost as well as his parents.

The older Confederados, much like the Polish on Milwaukee Avenue in northwest Chicago, continued the established ways of doing things. They exhibited their American side at every opportunity, sought out visiting Americans, listened to American records, spoke English, and cussed mightily in the vernacular. The language that is spoken is of the Old South. The regional differences of southern English seem to have blended together. Texas, Louisiana Delta, and Georgia linguistic differences are now almost gone. It seems likely that the language, which is not subject to the influences of U.S. radio and television, remains very close to that spoken before the Civil War.

There was great emphasis on good manners. Mother wanted us to be "refined." Family and home ties were important, for "blood is thicker than water, you know!" Guests were awarded extreme cordiality, and the crystal was always brought out in their presence.

Evenings at home frequently saw mother at the Steinway upright piano playing a variety of Brazilian concert pieces, along with some songs from antebellum days—"Red Wing," "Listen to the Mockingbird," "Dixie," Methodist hymns, and a few Stephen Foster favorites. Sometimes we picnicked on the banks of the Ipanema Lagoa (lake) behind our house.

The word *honor* was frequently heard. Honor your principles, your parents, your religion, and your debts. To question a man's word was to insult his honor. Storytelling talent was an important social asset. Humor and those skilled in its use were especially valued. A certain southernness seemed to color our lives all the time, and it fitted well with the cultural values of Brazil.

HOUSES WITH CHIMNEYS
DISCOVERED BY FAMOUS EXPLORERS

Once, in Ohio in the 1930s, I was asked by a cousin of mine how it felt to discard our native grass skirts for American clothing styles now that we had moved to the United States. The cousin had read about Brazil in school books and knew something of the country. Since the question was asked in all seriousness, I was left with the impression that there was an information gap in America about Brazil and especially about the Confederates who moved there.

It was just such a gap that the American Geographical Society tried to fill in 1918 when it sent an expedition to several South American countries. They knew they would find the Confederates there, for the famous explorer Sir Richard Burton had encountered them fifty years before, on his expedition to Brazil. He had been surprised at their numbers and had carefully noted that twenty-seven hundred had already arrived by 1867.

The society's explorers also knew how to find the transplanted southerners. They had only to look for houses with chimneys, for the Confederates who lived in the cooler parts of Brazil, such as Americana, Piracicaba, Campinas, or the state of Paraná, always built fireplaces in their houses. Some Brazilians copied the design, and such dwellings became known as American houses. Glass in the windows and sliding sashes were other distinguishing features. Brazilians in the outlying area usually had only storm shutters to keep out the elements. Some of the Confederado houses also featured fancy stoves from the U.S., which served to heat up the parlors where visitors were entertained. Other typical American features were the eaves, troughs, and guttering around the roofs.

The American Geographical Society, known for its courageous probings into the primitive portions of the world, sent the 1918 expedition to South America under the leadership of Dr. Alfred Coester. Outfitted with pith helmets, mosquito nets, and native bearers, the explorers searched the Brazilian countryside. They located the distinctive chimney-topped houses and found they contained the sizable number of Confederates that had been rumored to live in the area.

The expedition scientists photographed the "natives" and made field notes on these fierce Confederate warriors, just as they had done when they studied the Hotentots. They also photographed the houses, including the Hall Plantation home with its two-story veranda and picket fence. They sampled the Georgia watermelon and they carefully catalogued all their finds.

One of the Confederate, now Brazilian, natives told them that he had recently returned from the United States, where he had gone to establish his American citizenship (a pretty handy thing to have in those days, since it could keep one from being conscripted into the Brazilian army). Alas, the U.S. government had refused citizenship to the man, probably on the grounds that his parents and grandparents were technically still foreigners, Confederates, and not United States citizens. They had no record of a pardon being granted to them.

The explorers were given a tour of the prosperous plow factory and recorded that the Confederates traveled about in American-style, horse-drawn buckboards (called *troles* by the Brazilians).

The explorers wrote their findings in the April 1928 issue of the *Geographical Review.* It was a short, informative piece, excellent in its insights about the perseverance of the American culture transplanted overseas. But the racist, ethnocentric character of the paper of this learned society tells volumes about the imperialist feeling of the times. "The infusion of American blood in the Brazilian race was worth while," it bragged. The paper concentrated on the negative aspects. The Confederates were unhappy. They would have been better off had they stayed in Georgia during Reconstruction. They had made "small mark" upon Brazil. They had gone to the wrong place. "Burdened with debts, living in squalor, with broken-down bodies and discouraged hearts, they hated the nearby Italians." There was no opportunity in Brazil. On and on and on went the article, painting a moralizing picture of the folly of leaving the U.S.

There were no success stories, no mention of the big coffee, cane, and cotton plantations. In the six-page treatise, only one sentence was given to the thousands of Confederados who had moved to the cities of Brazil: "But in the cities to which the Americans mostly drift they add a most desirable element to Brazilian society into which they are likely to be promptly amalgamated."⁵ There are very few of these scientists around, it seems, who are willing to ignore their own culture in defining the rest of the world.

VINEGAR PIE IN LEMON COUNTRY

Like any resourceful people of agricultural heritage, the southern immigrants had no trouble raising enough meat, vegetables, and fruit to feed the family. Given the advantages of Americana's good soil and mild climate, they quickly set to work to reap the benefits of a good planting. Confederados had brought their "receipts" with them, and a mere glance at the black loam kicked up by walking across the fields was enough to remind them of the harvest to come.

The dishes were works of art. Corn bread, burgoo stew, chess pie, spoon bread, egg bread, crackling bread, and biscuits were among the delights. Corn continued to be the key product in most recipes, and there were rice dishes by the score. Buttermilk was a universal favorite, and one of my earliest memories is sweetened buttermilk at the breakfast table. Black-eyed peas, potatoes in a variety of ways, and southern fried chicken or roast beef were frequently in evidence.

Desserts were vinegar pie (though a juicy variety of lemons grew almost wild in everyone's back yard), ambrosia (orange slices mixed with coconut), custard, fruit pies, and ginger cake. This was followed by coffee in tiny cups. Every Confederado housewife had her collection of these beautiful cups. Southerners in the United States had been drinking their coffee this way since the French and Spanish introduced the product (as a tonic, originally) in the port of New Orleans in the 1700s.

In Americana, the colonists learned more about the diversity of southern cooking. Each had his regional dishes; the Louisianians, their rice and barbecues; the Tennesseans and Kentuckians, their burgoo; the Arkansans, their corn dodgers—all a delight to the senses.

With prosperity came cooks and servants, and the Brazilian cooks were not shy about introducing the immigrants to native dishes. The most mysterious substance to arrive at the table was mandioca flour, grainy, crunchy, and with little flavor. Our good-humored cook, who had that wonderfully Brazilian name Conceição (Conception), decided that she was the cultural ambassador to the American Confederados and set about to alter our tightly held culinary prejudices. She began by subtly attacking our breakfast habits. For example, when we asked for scrambled eggs, we got exactly what was ordered, with the addition of mandioca flour sprinkled liberally over the top. Early morning scrambled eggs buried in flour can rudely awaken you unless you are accustomed to it by years of training.

The colonists of course rebelled and counterattacked the kitchen help, gaining victories in some skirmishes, losses in others. But the process of amalgamating Confederate and Brazilian food had begun. Almost every dish, including desserts, had the blessing of mandioca added, altering the eating habits of first-, second-, and third-generation Confederados in a way that made a return to cornmeal dumplings difficult indeed. Brazilian mandioca has won out.

Mandioca was originally grown by the Amazonian Indians and introduced through them into the diets of the Portuguese, Africans, Spanish, Dutch, French, German, Italian, and now, American settlers. This root, which is the staple of Brazilian dinner tables, in the remote areas takes the place of corn and wheat in many breads, cookies, and cakes, though it has little of the consistency of corn or wheat. It is a symbol of the way the Indian culture intermingled with the Portuguese beginning in the sixteenth century. It was an easily grown, readily available, passive kind of substance that blended tastelessly with almost any kind of food, giving additional bulk at very low cost.

Had we known what mandioca really was, however, we might have resisted it more strenuously in those early days. The root in its natural state is quite bitter, and some varieties are poisonous. These must be soaked in a tub for several days so the prussic acid can be washed away. (The Indians used the poison as a valuable by-product, dipping their arrows into it and so adding to the killing power of their weapons.) The root is next set out in the sun to dry. Afterward, it is pounded in a large, heavy wooden receptacle with a blunt paddle until it achieves a

Five Confederados are shown, side by side, in a photo taken in 1910. Grandfather Harris is at left.

Harris family shown at their home in Americana, Brazil, a few years after the visit by Secretary of State Elihu Root. Left to right (standing): Gibson Harris (author's uncle); Maglin Harris (mother); Emma Thatcher Harris (grandmother); and Christina and her husband, Simeon Harris, the oldest son (aunt and uncle). Seated is the author's grandfather, John Wesley Harris, born in Meridian, Mississippi.

Maglin Harris, my mother, is here shown in her graduation picture. She received her diploma from the Confederado Teachers College in Campinas, Brazil, in 1918.

In 1939 David Riker, one of the original migrants of the Lansford Warren Hastings colony to the Brazilian jungle area, was living in comfortable retirement in this large, Portuguese-style house located on the banks of the Amazon River near Santarem. Riker (wearing dark coat) stands in the doorway with members of his family. Note the American Eagle that decorates the structure.

Watermelons, grown from American seed, were introduced by the Confederates into Brazil. They became so popular that the southerners were shipping as many as a hundred railroad carloads a day from the station at Americana to all parts of the country in the latter part of the nineteenth century. This photograph appeared in a São Paulo newspaper.

A postcard view of Americana about 1912 when the population was approximately 2,500. It is now a city of 120,000. The town was among the most progressive in Brazil. Note the automobile among the mules.

Americana is a neat, bustling city with a downtown area dominated by parks and wide streets. Gene Harter, the author's son, stands before one of the many monuments.

This is the country church on the Confederate cemetery grounds in Americana, as descendants leave after the service on a Sunday morning.

The services at the church on the Confederate cemetery grounds are well attended. Flags of Brazil, the Confederate States of America, and the United States are draped, side-by-side, over the alter.

U.S. Consul Eugene Harter, with U.S. presidential candidate Jimmy Carter, points out his mother's family listed on the Confederate monument in São Paulo, Brazil, in 1972. Grandmother Harris and his uncle are buried nearby on the same grounds. The event was telecast for U.S. television and covered by the Associated Press.

medium fine consistency. It is then strained through a sieve and roasted over a fire while being sprinkled gently with water.

It is the national dish, quite distinctive to Brazil, and any immigrant must come to terms with it. It is served as a dessert, fried with bacon pieces, over rice, over eggs, over green vegetables, and in candy. You learn to love it, or else.

By the mid-1930s, third-generation Confederados had settled into many Brazilian ways. Breakfasts consisted of native fruits and fresh, hard-crusted small loaves of bread (*pãozinhos*), with an American touch such as ham and eggs now and then. In 1935 on a visit to the interior we noticed, however, that some Brazilian restaurants in the vicinity of the Confederado settlements had taken to serving food cooked in the U.S. way. "Ham 'n Eggs" headed the menu of one small village *merceria* that had a restaurant in the back. "Mãe (we always used the Portuguese word for mother, even when speaking English), Look! American food!"

The store was located twenty miles from Americana, at an isolated crossroads. In the back behind the dry goods, tools, tin cans, and groceries was a small restaurant with four tables. The Portuguese owner, quickly spotting us as *Americanos*, pointed to the ham and egg feature on his menu. We ordered up and loved every bite.

ARE CONFEDERADOS AND THEIR CHILDREN AMERICANS?

Well into the twentieth century the Confederados in Brazil were still discussing the shabby treatment of southerners in the U.S. Despite the fact that Democrats had been returned to power with the election of President Grover Cleveland in 1884, no complete, unrestricted amnesty was ever issued.

The harrassment of the South contrasts with the friendly relationship between the United States and its defeated enemies, Germany, Italy, and Japan, soon after the end of World War II. No such era of good feeling existed following the Civil War. The Republicans had found a tried-and-true formula for getting elected. Their strategy was to remind the voters that it was the Grand Old party that had won the war against the Rebels. "Waving the bloody shirt" it was called. It reopened the war's wounds, but the tactic sent the faithful scurrying to the polls to vote for the one party that was not "soft on traitors."

However, a series of amnesty bills, many of them deliberately vague, gave the rights of citizenship to increasing numbers of the Confederacy's leaders. The last of these, passed in 1898, failed to make the pardon universal, and to this day, the situation has never been rectified.

In the Reconstruction era, the sight of the Confederate leaders exiling themselves to other countries seemed to anger the North, as noted in the September 26, 1865, issue of the *New York Observer*. The paper reported that "Attorney General Speed will not in future give consideration to applications for pardon from rebels not resident in this country. It is supposed that the effect of this will be perpetual expatriation in the cases of many of the 'extinguished' individuals formerly prominent in Jeff Davis' Confederacy."

When Lee surrendered to Grant at Appomattox, the terms included the awarding of parole to the defeated army troops. This was to protect the soldier from molestation, in return for which he would remove himself from the war and go home. But the paroles were not honored by the North, and the Confederate veterans could not transfer title to property or participate in some business activities until their status as complete citizens was returned. In addition, the Fourteenth Amendment kept them from holding state or federal office. The harassment, added to the economic conditions of the postwar South, made life there unbearable, especially to the youthful and ambitious. Ten years after the war southern poet Sidney Lanier wrote in a letter, "Perhaps you know that with us of the younger generation in the South since the war, pretty much the whole of life has been merely not dying."[6]

The state of Kentucky, neutral in the war but with a majority sympathetic to the South, chose to ignore the federal law when it made Simon Bolivar Buckner its governor even though he had not received a federal pardon. Not until 1957 were treason and conspiracy indictments against Buckner finally dismissed, when a circuit court in Kentucky exonerated him posthumously. In the same year other Confederate leaders from Kentucky, including John C. Breckinridge and John Hunt Morgan, were also posthumously exonerated.

Confederados have been supporters of the Democratic party in the United States even to this day. In the post–Civil War years they followed the events in America closely through the U.S. newspapers mailed to them. The papers frequently spoke of the violence that was flaring in the South as the Radical Republicans sought to maintain power. In 1874 Arkansas was engaged in its own civil war, with over two hundred killed. In the same year President Grant ordered General Sheridan to Louisiana to put down violence. In 1876, reports Hodding Carter, white South Carolinians were prepared, as a last resort, to engage in open civil war.[7]

According to the law in the United States, the child of an American couple is automatically a citizen of the U.S.A. no matter where the birth occurred. Confederate immigrants, however, could not be certain if their American citizenship had ever been restored. Those of their children who returned to the U.S. to live felt themselves in limbo. One woman, for example, came to the United States from Americana in the 1930s. Her parents had been in the McMullen colony that landed in Iguape in 1867, well before the rights of citizenship had been restored to the majority of southerners in the U.S. Some of the exiles had their citizenship returned to them, piecemeal, by the Congress under the May 22, 1872, general amnesty law, but this lady was uncertain if the law had applied to her parents. I once asked her if she was a citizen of the United States, and she answered, "I surely hope so, but sometimes I wonder!" Though she voted in every election and lived very much as a proper Mississippi lady, she had the gnawing feeling that she was a foreigner.

In the 1970s she telephoned the immigration service to get a clarification from Washington. "Confederate States of America? Hmm, let's see." There was a long pause. Then the functionary offered, "That's a foreign matter; ask the Department of State." She called the department, reached several officials, who shuffled her call around but never came up with a satisfactory answer. She was one of many southerners who felt a measure of satisfaction when General Robert E. Lee, traitor no more, received his citizenship at last in 1975.

The official seal of the city of Americana shows its American beginnings: the Confederate soldiers, the spinning wheel, the fortress, and the rendition of the Confederate battle flag. This city of 160,000 is now mostly populated with descendants of European immigrants, who arrived in the late nineteenth and early twentieth centuries.

FIVE

A Confederate Miscellany

U NLIKE the southerners they left behind in the United States, Brazil's Confederados remembered a prewar secessionist political leader more often than their wartime generals when it came time to name their children.

YANCEY, THE FAVORITE CONFEDERADO NAME

Before the Civil War, the name Yancey was synonymous with secession from the Union, for as some historians agree, it was Senator William Lowndes Yancey of Alabama who split the Union. His oratory, heard throughout the South, fanned the fires of secession. His was the voice of secession, heard everywhere. At every large gathering, at political conventions, in state houses, his opinions were heard, and he struck a chord with the southern listener. Now Yancey is almost unknown in the U.S. South, but the Confederados continue to honor him.

It wasn't that the Confederados did not hold their military commanders or other political leaders in high regard. However, when the stone monuments, the carved likenesses of Confederate generals that decorate every single courthouse lawn in the southern part of the United States, were being built, most Confederados had already left for Brazil. They didn't feel the same need as the southerners under Yankee occupation to express defiance to the North by building such memorials. Their gesture was made in moving away from their native land.

Moreover, the generals did not go to Brazil, but Yancey's sons, Ben and Dalton, did. They kept his memory alive, and his speeches were still quoted at length in Americana well into the twentieth century.

William Lowndes Yancey was a lover of horses, high style, and plantation living. He was born in South Carolina, but when he was very young, his father, a law associate of John C. Calhoun, died. His mother remarried and moved to New York state. Yancey attended Williams College in New England, then returned to his native South. A successful lawyer and newspaper editor, he went to Alabama and set up a plantation, managing his properties from his home in Montgomery. Unlike his father's associate, Calhoun, Yancey became convinced that the South was suffering at the hands of the industrializing North and that the only solution was separation.

In an era when nations beggared their neighbors by imposing protective tariffs, the North, too, joined the bandwagon by ramming through Congress a series of tariff measures designed to protect northern factories. Other countries reciprocated by imposing a tariff on cotton, America's dominant export and the South's life blood. Southerners were furious but impotent, for the North was able to outvote them in Congress.

William Lowndes Yancey refused to believe that the South must bow to the will of the North. He began to tell southerners that their future was dim if they remained in the Union. To remain subservient to the industrial North would mean economic ruin for the states of the South. He was for southern independence and would settle for no less than secession from the Union, and that was the message that he promulgated for almost two decades. After serving only one term, he resigned from the U.S. Congress, declaring that he was a southerner and that, as such, he would never again hold federal office.

Witnesses of the time gave a glowing description of his effective speaking style. He was by nature a quiet, courteous man, very neat in appearance and not given to florid gestures. He could command his audience for hours with the choice of his words and the power of his voice alone. He appeared everywhere in the South, at all major gatherings, and he invariably held his audiences spellbound.

He was convinced that the North had long determined to destroy the South for its own industrial gain. Though Jefferson Davis was his ally for a short while, Yancey soon found himself running ahead of southern sentiments and being judged too extreme. By 1861, however, the tariffs, John Brown's raid at Harper's Ferry, the election of Abraham Lincoln, and a myriad of other unifying events, had brought the South in step with Yancey. Southerners were at last ready to follow where he led. Lifelong opponents of secession united behind him in withdrawing from the Union.

Historians have tended to downplay Yancey's role during the Civil War. But in 1902, William G. Brown attempted to restore some of the luster to the name of this man who held few high offices and left few written words but had the attention of the southern body politic. While serving as an influential member of the Confederate Senate, William L. Yancey clashed frequently with President Jefferson Davis, who was, at times, a hard man to get along with. He complained to Davis because the Alabama brigades were led by officers from other states, a situation that mortified the Alabamian. Davis also incurred Yancey's ire when he refused to give Dalton Yancey a commission in the Confederate army, despite the fact that the young man held the rank of captain in the Alabama state militia.

When Jefferson Davis was made president of the new Confederate States of America it had been William L. Yancey who was chosen to present Davis to the cheering throngs that filled Fountain Square in Montgomery, Alabama, the first capital city of the new nation. His introduction contained his most memorable phrase in a long career of eloquent statements: "The man and the hour have met!" One of the first acts of the new nation, even before it was fully organized, was to send Yancey and two other prominent southerners to Europe to secure recognition for the Confederacy—a difficult and ultimately unsuccessful mission.

He died on his plantation near Montgomery on July 28,

1863, and was buried in Oakwood Cemetery. Had he lived longer, many Confederados believe, he would have been the natural leader of the exodus to South America. With his talent for persuasion, he might have single-handedly emptied the South of its population and sent them into Brazil.

As it was, there were plenty of Yanceys in Americana. Ben Yancey lived out his life in the colony as a planter and real estate investor. Dalton later moved back to Alabama. There were also Yancey Hall, Yancey Harris, Yancey Jones, Yancey Jones II, Leonardo Yancey Jones, Yancey Matthews, and many others. So numerous were the Yanceys that even Brazilians knew the origins of the name. The Yancey I knew most about was Yancey Harris, second eldest of my uncles. He was a man as intense and fiery as his namesake, with a mind of his own. He was twenty-two in 1918 when he broke the Confederado code by marrying a lovely, tall bronze-skinned Brazilian girl, Leonilda Novães Lima, whom he had met at MacKenzie University in São Paulo. They had one daughter, Odette. Over the years, probably to distinguish him from the host of other Yanceys, we had taken to calling him Uncle Granville, his middle name.

Brazilian, Gilberto Freyre, whose excellent insights have been widely read and studied all over the world, explains the Yancey phenomenon by the love of politics fostered in both the U.S. South and Brazil by plantation life. "Romanticism," wrote Freyre, "was one of the general psychological effects of the plantation and slavery system upon Brazil. And with romanticism, there was fondness of rhetoric, common to Brazilians and to Anglo-Americans of the two areas of the New World where slavery flourished with its most dramatic vigor: the South of the United States and the sugar and coffee regions of Brazil. As in the South of the United States, in those Brazilian regions rhetoric became 'not only a passion,' but, as Cash points out in his famous book 'a primary standard of judgment, the sine qua non of leadership.' This love of oratory was associated in Brazil as in the southern region of the United States, with 'the love of politics.'"[1] As in the South of William Lowndes Yancey, oratory could move mountains in Brazil.

PROTESTANTS IN A CATHOLIC COUNTRY

Whether the Confederados brought the Protestant religion to Brazil or whether the U.S.-based religious organizations merely took advantage of the southern presence in Brazil to establish missions there could be a source of conjecture. The historical record shows that with the importation of only a few U.S. missionaries, the Protestant church in Brazil has grown to a membership of many millions, the largest in South America. Not only churches but many schools were established as well, and these have had a profound effect on Brazil's educational system. Blanche Weaver, who generally minimizes the impact of the Confederados on Brazilian culture, wrote:

> There are two fields . . . in which the North Americans did make significant contributions to Brazil. The permanent establishment of missionary work of the southern branches of the major Protestant churches in the United States can be attributed to the activities of these colonial groups. This not only marked the beginning of the steady growth of evangelical churches, but also led to the establishment of schools under North American sponsorship. Consequently the contributions of southern immigrants to the religious and educational life of the country were far greater than might be expected from such a limited number of people.[2]

In some cases, it was the ministers who exhorted their congregations to emigrate and led the groups that settled in Brazil. Grandfather's foster father, the Reverend Junius C. Newman, gave up his church and plantation near Meridian and, in partnership with his neighbor the Reverend W. C. Emerson, organized a group to move to Brazil. Emerson, on arrival, took advantage of his religious position and his contacts in the U.S. (he had been a college president as well as a minister) to found a newspaper. He mailed the *Emigration Reporter* to one and all back in the United States, hoping to inspire them to join him in Brazil.

The disaffection that permeated the southern states during the war and Reconstruction reached even into the churches. Many ministers joined the Confederate army, some achieving high rank. Lieutenant General Leonidas Polk, for example, had

left his position as bishop of the Episcopalian church to join the
army. He served with distinction, leading large forces into battle, until he was killed at the Battle of Pine Mountain. Most
ministers became chaplains rather than fighting men, but their
support for the cause of the South was undiminished by their
noncombatant status. One such leader was General A. T.
Hawthorne, who was a lay preacher in the Baptist church. He
brought over a group of immigrants and himself leased a small
plantation near Rio de Jameiro, naming it Dixie Island. Hawthorne later returned to the United States to enter into the
ministry full time, but he never forgot his Brazil experience. He
devoted his efforts in the remainder of his lifetime to mustering
support for Baptist missions to Brazil. Others, likewise, established churches for their own groups of settlers that became the
nuclei of the evangelical missions that followed.

Brazil accepted the missionaries. There was no nationwide
outcry against these aggressive men who openly declared that
theirs was the true religion and that their listeners should aban-
don the state-supported Roman Catholic faith of their
forefathers. However, some restrictions were imposed on the
new Protestants. For example, by law their houses of worship
were to be limited in size and devoid of the outward trappings of
a church, such as a steeple, towers, gongs, stained-glass windows, and other come-hither attractions to those seeking organized faith.

The Confederados were fortunate to have arrived at a time
when the Brazilian Catholic church had its hands full holding
on to its interests in that country. A movement to separate
church and state and to increase religions freedom for all faiths
had begun in 1824 with the agreement with Britain to allow her
subjects to worship freely. British subjects were allowed to have
their own cemeteries, to conduct funerals, and to perform all
their rituals. It was the first break in a ban against Protestantism
and other religions that Brazil had maintained for 250 years.

As part of the inducements to Confederates, the emperor
promised them freedom of religion, but occasionally local authorities would make things difficult. The Brazilian people accepted the difference in religion despite the harangues of the

church authority against the "Protestant heretics." The Confederate cemetery in Americana came into being because in the early days of the settlement a local official denied the settlers the right to bury their dead in the municipal graveyard. They responded by creating the burial grounds on the Bookwalter property, where it remains to this day.

Charles Freligh, a Brazilian diplomat who is currently living in retirement in West End, North Carolina, and whose family migrated from Louisiana to Brazil in 1870, had studied the ease with which the southerners introduced their Protestantism into Brazil. "We merged into Brazilian society by intermarriage and acceptance," he said. "In this, we were aided by the kindly nature of the Brazilian people. Confederate Protestantism, in the midst of a Catholic majority, was tolerated because the Portuguese people never were as fanatical as were the Hispano-Americans. In addition, the Brazilians were strongly influenced by the precepts of Auguste Comte's Positivism. The Brazilian flag itself bears the imprint of Positivist thought in its motto, 'Ordem e Progresso.' (Order and Progress)."

Blanche Weaver emphasized the role of both the Freemasons and the Positivists of that time in Brazil. "The Freemasons attracted not only the religiously dissatisfied but also Catholics in good standing, clerical as well as lay. Although the number of Positivists was small, the ideas which they advanced were ones on which the Protestant faith could readily build—individual liberty, the constant development of human personality, and the importance attached to morality and the development of a feeling of responsibility and justice. The efforts of the Jesuits to eliminate these and other forces which threatened Catholic supremacy led to conflicts over questions of the relation between church and state which were not settled until 1891 when separation of the two was achieved in the fundamental law of the republic."[3]

The tolerant attitude of the Brazilians was widely known in the American South, and religious freedom was one of the attractions that inspired many of the colonists. The Confederados were a mixed breed. Some were almost fanatic in their religious pursuits, while others were merely tolerant. But almost all were happy over the presence of ministers of the faith to marry, baptize, bury, and console their fellow colonists.

Bellona Smith Ferguson, in an article in the *Times of Brazil,* December 18, 1936, described the preachers and the effect of the church on the Confederados, still homesick in the years following their arrival in São Paulo:

> . . . We found out that Parson Quillen was preaching near Guananha. Our first visit over there was by water or by an old trail over three mountains but now we learned a new trail that had only one mountain—even that trail was a tough proposition, for unless we started early we could not get there on time. . . . Quillen was much above the average preacher, as a learned man, and brought his very superior collection of books and we sat spellbound under his eloquent preaching. Our "meeting house" was in the shade of a tree with rude seats . . . but the lessons were just as interesting and the hymns just as sweet and we made the woods ring with "There is a Happy Land" and all the rest of those Sunday School songs. . . . I made up my mind to join the Church at the first opportunity, which came to pass afterward at the Campo [the Confederate cemetery], while Parson Newman was preaching in an old-fashioned "venda" [small store] on the roadside that led from the Campo to Santa Barbara.

EMANCIPATION DAY IN BRAZIL

May 13, 1888, was an important date in Brazil, for on that day the slaves were freed. But in the Confederado colony the event passed almost without notice. There were no celebrations like those that occurred elsewhere in Brazil. As was their habit, the slaves reported for work for the same plantation owners, living in the same small dwellings set well away from the big house. They now received wages, but in exchange they were required to pay rent for their houses and to buy the food they ate. The sounds of sawing wood, horses' hooves, and the villagers' greetings to one another were the same as the day before. In general, relations between former slaves and their former owners were cordial, becoming even more so as they jointly experienced the economics of freedom from bondage. A stranger passing through the area would not have noticed anything different, unless he had questioned the ex-slaves, who were rejoicing quietly. Some of the Confederados grumbled, "Now we can discharge them if they don't feel like working," but none were turned out. Every hand was needed to take care of the growing coffee plantations.

One of the aspects that bound the Confederados' former slaves closely to their old community was their new religion. Many had been converted to the Protestant faith by Reverend Newman and the other missionaries now in abundance. In a predominantly Catholic country, a Protestant stood apart like a zebra in a pack of mules. Protestants liked to stay together; Protestant ex-slaves were no different. Also, quite a few of the slaves had learned to speak English to accommodate the Confederados who still struggled with Portuguese. Some adopted the names of their masters.

It gives one pause to use the expression "kindly slave-owner," a contradiction in terms by our standards. But there were those Confederados who treated their slaves with more compassion than others. One of those was Edwin Britt. The story is told about the unfortunate young slave Manuel. Manuel had enlisted in the Brazilian army on the promise that, if he fought against Paraguay, he would be given his freedom on discharge. But when the time came, the promise was not kept. Instead he was jailed by a shady official, who then offered him for sale.

The slave, who had become ill, was in despair. Along came Confederate migrant Edwin Britt who bought him and helped him to regain his health before he joined the work force of Britt's fazenda. It is not recorded whether Manuel remained in the status of slave while working for the Confederado; perhaps the grateful slave never brought the issue up. He took Britt for his surname, however, and on the heirless Edwin Britt's deathbed, he willed the entire plantation to Manuel.[4]

And so they stayed on, these English-speaking, Protestant, American-named former slaves, and they too brought a measure of cultural change to Brazilian life around them. Grandfather had six slaves who took the Harris name. When he sold out his half interest in the coffee plantation to his brother-in-law, Simeon Thatcher, and moved fifty miles away to Piracicaba, he tried to stay in touch with them. From time to time, the family has encountered descendants of these Brazilian slaves. Just recently (August 1984) a distant cousin in Rio de Janeiro, Betty Thomas de Oliveira, wife of a Brazilian congressman, wrote me to inquire about one of them, Sebastiana Harris. Sebastiana was one of the founders of the First Baptist Church of Rio de Janeiro, which recently celebrated its one hundredth anniversary.

ELIHU ROOT COMES FOR A FRIENDLY VISIT

Confederado Charles MacFadden still tells this story about his father: Having invited a visiting American to have supper with them at their plantation near Americana, the MacFadden family seated itself around the table, bowing their heads in expectation of the elder MacFadden's ritual blessing of the food. Instead, the father suddenly looked up and addressed the visiting stranger, "From what state did you say you came?" The man, startled, revealed that he was from a northern state. Whereupon MacFadden pushed himself away from the table and left the room. He would still not break bread with a Yankee, even forty years after the end of the Civil War. Nor was his an isolated case.

As we have noted, little has been written about the migration of Confederados, but those articles that exist usually mention the visit of U.S. Secretary of State Elihu Root to Americana in 1906. The source of these stories of his encounter with the Confederados is recorded in his biography, written by Ambassador Philip Jessup, who wrote it from Root's description of the event. The account has gone a long way in misshaping the history of the southerners who chose life in Brazil. One can only speculate on the secretary of state's motivation in creating his fairy tale. It was propaganda, served up with a dose of crocodile tears.

The reason for his journey to Brazil was a meeting of the Pan American Union. At the end of the conference, which was held in Rio, his hosts scheduled a rail tour of the countryside in the beautiful state of São Paulo, with visits to the prosperous coffee plantations. Coffee was the nation's most important export, and the United States, its best customer. One of the stops was at the railroad station at Americana, situated in the heart of the abundant coffee fields. Many of the coffee plantations were owned or managed by the Confederados.

Grandfather Harris was fifty years old at that time. He was somewhat younger than most of the other original migrants. Their memories of the United States were hazy. Almost none of them had gone back for a visit, and they were solidly Brazilianized after forty years. Most had prospered; many had served in the state militia. Some, like Johnnie MacNight, mayor of Americana, had become important political figures in the area. They had founded hospitals, a university and had even built their own small city. They were as firmly implanted at that time as the Irish in Boston or the Norwegian farmers in Minnesota.

Grandfather Harris stood on the railroad platform with Uncle Simeon, who had just received his degree in engineering from MacKenzie College in São Paulo. They clustered with four-hundred other Confederados as the special train bearing the secretary of state and his party approached. Some, like Grandfather, had learned to swallow their bitterness. They were ready to receive Root with the courtesy befitting his high position. As was their custom at festive occasions, they hung three flags high over the building, the Confederate in the center, the United States and the Brazilian flags on either side. The station was a rather imposing two-story brick building, designed to resemble most U.S. stations of the time.

Root, staring from the train window, hardly knew what to expect. The U.S. consul from Santos, who was riding with him on the train, assured him that these natives were friendly. They celebrated the Fourth of July faithfully, and besides—reaching for the secretary's political instincts—many still had contacts with voters back in the U.S.

The party, consisting of Root, his assistants, the Brazilian minister of foreign affairs, and the governor of São Paulo, alighted from the train and shook hands with the Confederados. As he passed among them, the secretary exchanged small talk, noting that all of them, even some of the grandchildren, spoke to him in English.

He agreed to address the crowd, but as Grandfather remembered it, he seemed at a loss for words. The weight of being secretary of state suddenly fell very heavily upon him. He noted the Confederate flag. What could he say? Were these people expecting an apology for the Reconstruction policies of his fellow Republicans? Should he invite them back to America— even after forty years—and thereby insult the Brazilian government officials who were with him?

Root, took the only way out of the situation. He said a lot without actually saying anything. He spoke a few platitudes, friendly banter, thanks for the hospitality, and then he hopped back on the train, which quickly, to his relief, drew him away from the scene.

The incident stuck in Root's mind like a burr in his shoe. The sight of the proud Confederados was an assault on his patriotic, Yankee feelings. Twenty-five years later, he attempted to settle the account in describing the scene to his biographer. Root's story is as apocryphal as the fable of Washington's cutting down of the cherry tree. It combined the elements of Yankee wishful thinking with the unlikelihood that an American diplomat would advise his countrymen to stay away from the United States, since they wouldn't "fit in" any more.

Here is what Jessup wrote:

> Secretary of State Root had an experience which after twenty years he still could not describe without a break in his voice and tears in his eyes. A request was received that the train be stopped at a little station known as "American City." There, after the Civil War, had settled one of those small groups of southerners who had felt that exile was preferable to continuing to live under the iron heel of the "damnyankees." Most of them were from Alabama. They had settled down, intermarried with the Brazilians and were eking out a meager agricultural existence. It was after dark when the train stopped at the little shack of a station several miles from the town. The whole population was assembled, old white bearded survivors of the original exodus from Alabama; their full grown sons; women with babies in

their arms, standing in a mass looking up at the cabinet officer from their old fatherland, their faces lighted by flickering torchlight and lanterns. Their aged spokesman said they wanted his advice about returning to the United States. Root was deeply moved as he advised them not to return; they would be strangers in a new South with little chance to fit back into their former life; many of their children spoke only Portuguese; they were committed to the land of their adoption. The old men wept and the women wept, and the torchlight glittered on their streaming faces as the train pulled out of the station, the Secretary of State of the United States standing on the rear platform, tears running down his cheeks unchecked.[5]

Root, who claimed to have left in a hail of tears, was the last high official from Washington ever to visit the colony until the accidental visit of Jimmy Carter in 1972. Down through the years, however, an occasional U.S. consul would stop by to keep up on the activities of the rebels.

THE HALL PLANTATION IN BRAZIL

Confederado Hervey Hall constructed a duplicate of his lovely Georgia plantation on the Capivari Road, in the community of Retiro (now a suburb of Americana), where many Confederate families had settled, including the Wrights, Steagalls, Mac-Knights, Pyles, MacAlpines, and Tanners. Crowning the estate was a spacious, typical Old South mansion. It was a home designed for visitors. A traveler could stay overnight in the comfortable bedrooms and stroll through the manicured gardens. Several buildings, including the cotton ginhouse, tobacco-curing barn, and slave cabins, surrounded the big house, serving the plantation economy. It even had its own church building. Only the coffee-drying pallets gave it a foreign appearance, distinguishing it ever so slightly from the larger plantations of the American Old South.

The neighbors, some with pride, others with envy, pointed out to visitors the lovely house and grounds. Grandfather Harris in his youth lived nearby. He described Hervey Hall as a courtly gentleman who was kind to the children in the neighborhood but seldom took his mind off the management of his plantation. Hall was blessed with an acute business sense, and he knew how to grow cotton. He began making money almost from the day he arrived in Brazil. Far from the reach of the U.S. federal government, he had reconstructed his prewar way of life. But he was haunted by tragic events. Intensely religious since the death of his wife at war's end at their home in Columbus, Georgia, he sought comfort in his work and in the church community in his new surroundings. The Reverend Newman, in whose home Grandfather resided, was his closest friend.

After the war Hall had sold his possessions for ten cents on the dollar, had gathered up his four grown children (the two boys were veterans of the Confederate army, members of Lee's forces in Virginia), and in May 1866 had left for faraway Brazil. To forget the past, Hall immersed himself in his labors. The memories of his wife, of the war, and of his lost happy home in Georgia were a heavy burden.

The move was the tonic he was looking for. "I have never seen such prolific soil!" he exulted. "Everything grows as if by magic. . . . in less than two years we will have paid for this place from the proceeds."[6] Hall enjoyed writing back to the newspapers of his home state, describing his life in this new country. Balmy Brazil was a place where a man could enjoy long summer evenings all year long. His advice was to bring enough working capital to set up properly; two thousand dollars is the figure he used. He warned off the lazy. Be prepared to work with your hands, he cautioned. Through the Georgia papers, he recruited blacksmiths, house builders, furniture makers, wagon makers, and other technicians to join the São Paulo colony. "Fifteen dollars here I consider worth as much as twenty-five dollars in the States," he would repeat joyously.[7]

But for Hall, it all came to naught. One day in October 1877, eleven years after he had arrived in this strange land, he was shot dead by Jess Wright, the Texas cowboy, in a field near his home. There were no witnesses, but it was surmised that the shooting had followed an argument between the two men. Judith Jones recounts the story that a feud between the two came to a climax over Hall's shooting of one of the cowboy's mules that had wandered into Hall's plantation and was tramp-ling his cotton fields. In a rage, Wright apparently approached Hall demanding satisfaction. Within minutes Hall lay dead.[8]

After saying goodbye to his family, Wright fled the colony. Before nightfall a posse of Confederados and members of the Brazilian State Guard came looking for him, but Wright had caught a ride on a passing train and was in the port city of Santos, one hundred miles away, by the next morning. From there he caught a ship to New Orleans, safely out of reach.

The Confederates were stunned. They tried to console Hall's children. Both families were prominent. The Wrights had their friends and the Halls had theirs, and the ugly incident marred relations within the colony for many years. Things were especially unpleasant for those who helped Mrs. Wright and the children go to Texas to join her fugitive husband, now employed as a lawman. The belief was that Jess Wright was a gunslinger who had learned to use his six-shooter too well dur-ing the Civil War. Charlie, Hall's eldest son, planned to hunt Wright down in Texas to settle the score. His brother, George, finally persuaded him to drop the matter and let the Hall family begin life anew on the plantation.

Charlie, an energetic man like his father, took over the enterprise and made it prosper. Like many of the Brazilian Confederados, he raised a large family. As Blanche Weaver wrote of him "His spacious white-columned house with its wide verandas was the center of social life of the community. Minis-ters were invited to stay in his house and a church was built on his land. His hospitality served not only to lessen the loneliness of the young missionaries but also to encourage proper matches for his daughters."[9] Five of his nine daughters married mission-ary preachers from the United States.

Charlie Hall died in 1910 after suffering a fall at his home. The Hall Plantation existed until 1917, gradually diminishing in size as the city limits of Americana expanded and finally encircled the property. That year, at the death of Elizabeth, Charlie's wife, the mansion house was sold to Candido Cruz, a prosperous pharmacist in Americana. His wife converted the spacious home into a school, which continues in operation.

The sale of the aging plantation house also marked the beginning of the end for the church that the Halls had built on their property. It had become the ivy-covered Protestant Church of Americana, serving the entire community and conducting all services in English. It survived for a while, but the diminishing number of Confederates finally could not justify its existence, and it closed its doors. Today, only the chapel at the Confederate cemetery still remains as the "official" church of the Confederate descendants in Americana. As for the Halls, they slowly scattered in all directions down through the years, Brazilianized themselves, and receded into the vast society of that country.

THE HOMESICK ENGLISHMAN AND HIS COUNTRY ESTATE

In 1973 while I was serving as United States Consul in São Paulo, my wife, Dorothy, and I received an invitation to spend the weekend at the fazenda of Carson and Ellen Geld, whose pleasant company we had enjoyed many times during our tour of Brazil. By coincidence, Ellen and Dorothy had both lived in Mansfield, Ohio, early in their lives, where their parents had nearby farms. We welcomed the opportunity to pay another visit to an area where we knew the Confederados had lived a hundred years before. It was not far from Campinas, Mother's home in her childhood. Throughout her life she called herself a Campineira.

The Gelds were professional agriculturists, having come to Brazil at a relatively young age, direct from Cornell University's School of Agriculture. Ellen's father, the novelist Louis Bromfield, a world traveler, had developed an interest in Brazil's vast productive farmlands through his fascination with soil conservation and new farming techniques. He bought a plantation in partnership with several wealthy Brazilian investors because it reminded him of his own Malabar Farm back in Ohio. There were the same rolling hills, woods, springs, and marshlands. "My kind of country. This was the place. I was at home!"[10] he exclaimed.

The job of managing the plantation was given to Carson and Ellen, and they made a success of it. Later they bought and developed their own plantation in the same neighborhood, and there they were, still in Brazil twenty years later, testimony to the attraction of the country and its agriculture to emigrants from America.

Driving out to the Gelds' place we passed Brazilian Malabar, a marvelous estate, exactly as Bromfield had described it in his book *From My Experience*. The manor house with its stables was set amid lovely grounds at the end of a long driveway lined with eucalyptus trees at the edge of a river and marsh. The house had developed over the years with additions at either side, it was built of indigenous materials and whitewashed to a sparkle. Nearby were a large cattle shed and administrative buildings for the farm's management staff. The setting had been perfectly planned, with charming touches like the wide veranda, cool shrubbery, orchids, hibiscus, oleanders, palms, and much semitropical growth extending in all directions.

Our pleasant visit at the Geld house took us away from the turmoil of busy São Paulo, a city of twelve million people and much pollution. At night, as we strolled, we looked at the clear sky, the stars fairly popping out. They twinkled with a brilliance that cut through the clean air. It must have been this sight that helped ease the Confederados' pain of separation from their loved ones in America.

Bromfield enjoyed the natural opulence of the plantation, not unexpectedly, for he had lived in expensive surroundings most of his adulthood. He had achieved literary success early in life and had lived in Europe for many years, mostly in France. In buying the property he was getting not only a profitable farm but a baronial estate designed by someone of impeccable taste—an Englishman, he was told. He wrote of how he learned of the former owner.

> Carlito said, "The Englishman planted the trees." At one side there was a small canal of clear, swift-flowing water which fed a small lake with an island. . . . Mango trees grew everywhere and on the far side there were two more avenues of gigantic eucalyp-

tus trees. . . . the house had the charm that touches all houses that seem to have grown out of the very earth, generation by generation. . . . In the largest room which had a curious inexplicable Anglo-Saxon air, I made a very interesting discovery. There was a large library of English books revealing the taste of some owner who was no longer there. Mostly they were by H. Rider Haggard, Sir Oliver Lodge, Mrs. Humphrey Ward and other writers of the late Victorian period. When I commented upon the strangeness of such a library deep in the Brazilian countryside, Carlito said, "They belong to the Englishman," and I learned that years earlier the place had been the property of an English planter and banker who raised polo ponies and hunters. What became of him, whether he was alive or dead, no one seemed to know but the news seemed to clear up many things . . . the avenue of eucalyptus planted by a homesick Englishman as if to recall the great avenue of elms or oaks leading up to the big country houses in England. . . . a homesick Englishman had clearly attempted to recreate the damp cool beauties of the English gardens and countryside. . . . the 'tea' turned out to be an enormous meal, pastries, cakes. . . . there was coffee and tea and milk and small sandwiches (perhaps a custom left behind by the Englishman).[11]

Louis Bromfield was not only a skilled novelist but a good anthropologist as well. In this instance, however, he was led astray by the Brazilians in the area. The Paulistas made little distinction between Englishman, Yankee, or Confederate. They couldn't tell them apart. The "Englishman" of such perfect taste and obvious wealth was, in fact, a Confederado, now deceased, who had made his millions and had taken to raising horses, then moved to his residences in Rio de Janeiro and São Paulo in his retirement years.

This Confederado had lost everything to Sherman's marauders. He had scraped together passage to Brazil, surviving for a time by operating a bakery and coffeehouse. Then, remembering his plantation days, he set out for the interior, looking for cheap, good soil to establish his new plantation. By oxcart and foot he found his way to the Americana area where he began from scratch. Starting as a simple dirt farmer, he had operated with a few slaves who later, after gaining their freedom, became his paid workmen.

What Bromfield had mistakenly bought was not a baronial

estate but a southern plantation lovingly reimplanted, with its acres numbering in the thousands, its landscaped grounds—including seeds and plants imported from Alabama—and its display of the wealth of its Confederate owner. It was one of many established by Confederados in that area near Americana in south central Brazil that would have made the home folks back in the "Reconstructing" U.S. South proud.

Bromfield acknowledged his error in a footnote.

> I have recently discovered the true identity and a part of the history of "the Englishman" and at the same time discovered how greatly country gossip, hearsay and tradition can distort the truth. Actually the "Englishman" was a Brazilian citizen, American by blood, a baker by profession, and one of the descendants of a whole migration of Americans from the Southern States who left their country at the time it was invaded by the scoundrelly carpetbaggers of the North. . . . their presence in Brazil accounts for the fact that in many great Brazilian families today there exist names such as Washington, Lee and Jefferson. The former owner became known as "the Englishman" in the countryside simply because he spoke English. He was a great horse breeder and fancier.[12]

THE FAMILY

Records of the migrants to Brazil are sparse. In most cases, a researcher is forced to rely mainly on information stuffed inside family Bibles. This material says little or nothing about the details of the settlers' daily existence. However, these family records are invaluable for their listing of those who returned to the United States, of those who stayed on the plantations, of who married and when and to whom.

A study of the records of forty of the Confederate families reveals a desire to remain in Brazil, even when wealth makes it possible to visit the U.S. regularly. It is also evident that the settlers tried to marry within the Confederado community whenever possible. In my own family, on the Thatcher side, the second generation all married other U.S. settlers. In the third generation, there were some marriages with Brazilians of Portuguese descent, and more are evident in the fourth generation. My mother promised her parents that she would marry an

American. Although she had several Brazilian admirers, she kept her pledge. Those who defied the code were sometimes ostracized, left out of family gatherings and made to bear the brunt of hard feelings, at least for a while. Only one of the eight children of *Derby* survivors Calvin and Isabel MacKnight married a Portuguese Brazilian. In the third generation, none of the eleven children of Wilber and Caroline MacKnight married Brazilians of Portuguese descent. Emigrants Henry and Delia Steagall had eleven children in Brazil, and only one married outside the group. But gradually the ban on such marriages weakened, and more Portuguese names were introduced into the family trees.

The family bibles also reveal the tendency of Confederados to have large families. Great Aunt Dora Thatcher, for example, had eighteen children, most of whom migrated to São Paulo or Rio de Janeiro. None are recorded as returning to the United States, though. Despite the relatively large size of the Thatcher side of the family, one anthropologist from a U.S. university listed the Thatchers among "Families That Disappeared." His estimate that only two thousand Confederates moved to Brazil was also well off the mark.[13] Andrew and Eliza Thatcher's descendants now number in the hundreds, thanks to the continuing tendency toward large families. They are among the one hundred thousand U.S. Confederate descendants scattered throughout the vast country of Brazil.

THE COWBOYS

Americana and the Confederado-populated towns nearby had their wild west saloons, the most popular of which was the Lone Star on the outskirts of Santa Barbara. Cowboys (pronounced "K'boy" in Brazil) have long been heroes to Brazilians, who have been fed a steady stream of western comic strips and movies through the years. In 1971 after I was appointed consul in São Paulo, I brought along my Chevrolet sedan, which had Texas license plates, relics of my previous assignment at the U.S. embassy in Mexico City. When I drove through downtown São Paulo the plates almost stopped traffic. Pedestrians waved and smiled, shouting "K'boy! K'boy!"

The Confederados brought their cultural baggage with them. One of the manifestations was the armaments they displayed and used. Brazilians, were amused—and sometimes frightened—by the colony's supply of rifles, revolvers, and shotguns. This prominent display of weaponry gave the immigrants a Wild West look, and they did not hesitate to use the guns against man or animal.

Uncle Frank Thatcher, known for his prowess in bagging the deer that abounded in western São Paulo state, always had a revolver at his side when he visited the Santa Barbara saloon. My mother knew him well, for he always made a fuss over her when she was a little girl. He could charm the birds out of the trees when sober. After drinking the local alcoholic beverage, pinga (a form of rum), he would politely excuse himself from the bar rail, saunter outside, mount his horse, and ride at full gallop through the front door of the establishment shooting his revolver in the air all the while.

Needless to say, this made him quite unpopular with the bar patrons, not to mention the people in the nearby neighborhood, many of whom threw themselves to the ground when the shooting started. There was much crawling around, shutters banging closed, cries of "Maria!" "Por amor de Deus!" and "You bastard!" After firing his gun Uncle Frank would trot out the door and head for home. Since Uncle Frank was a major and the ranking officer in the military establishment, the Guarda Civil of Santa Barbara, no one raised a hand against him.

TWENTIETH-CENTURY CONFEDERATES IN THE AMAZON JUNGLE

Let us look again at the hardy band of Confederate families who went into the Amazon jungle, away from the contact with the Yankee. A surprising number prospered, a tribute to their perseverance and adaptability. Those who stayed had more than survival in mind. They were also aware of the potential rewards. Most had planned carefully, taking with them the machinery and working capital necessary to begin a large enterprise such as a plantation. They knew in advance the difficulties of settling in such surroundings. They had heard of the snakes so large that they could swallow a pig and the high humidity that was conducive to healthy plant life but hard for humans to bear.

But as for so many migrants elsewhere in the world, the main obstacle was adaptation and cross-cultural communication, the difficulty of living within a starkly different society, speaking a different language. A few of the Confederates were not prepared for the culture shock. Balthazar Nelius of Alabama was in the first group to settle in Santarém. As Thomas E. Griffin pointed out in the English-language *Brazil Herald*, Nelius was a bootmaker from Alabama who learned the hard way that few residents of the Amazon area wore shoes. These *caboclos* (peasants) showed no discomfort in walking around in bare feet in the warm surroundings. With his unmarketable skill, surrounded by natives he could barely understand, and suffering from persistent tropical fever and dysentery, Nelius hastily found his way back to Alabama. Griffin added, "Not only were the Portuguese language and the Amazonian culture alien to them, even fellow colonists were isolated from one another by living far apart."[14]

Women of the colony felt the isolation most severely. The Platt family, who had lived in a close-knit rural setting in the South, found isolation in the Amazonian rain forest almost unbearable. The only break from Mrs. Platt's household work occurred when her husband would hitch the four brown work-horses to the oversized farm wagon and take her and the children for an all-too-infrequent Sunday visit with a nearby Confederate immigrant family. The visits seemed to give the family the strength to cope with the unnerving aspects of their unfamiliar surroundings.

In spite of the problems, most of the Confederates stayed. The colonization of the Amazon area by the followers of Lansford Warren Hastings was an impressive achievement. Fellow Confederados from southern Brazil spoke in admiration of their fortitude in settling into Amazonia—which to us seemed a forbidding place. Theirs might have been the fate of a group of Germans who attempted to settle in similar territory in Amazonia, in the region of Ucayali across the Peruvian border.

Euclides da Cunha, the Brazilian writer, wrote this hyper-bolic account of them: "The colony became paralyzed, stag-nant, among the splendors of the forest. It was reduced to rudimentary crops which hardly sufficed for their consump-tion." The colonists, as da Cunha describes them, "went na-tive," and the survivors and their heirs could not be distin-guished from the Indians in the forest around them. When the prefect of nearby Huánuco visited the colony in 1870, he was astounded and deeply moved; the colonists came to him, ragged and famished, begging for bread and clothing to cover their nakedness. Another visitor reported that he "still saw the col-ony in the same somber colors five years later." When a Brazil-ian army colonel visited the Germans thirty years later, he reported their condition as "horrifying." Da Cunha wrote: "Deep in the wilds the primitive colonists and their degenerate progeny writhed, victims of a hopeless fanaticism, the dolorous slothfulness of penances, praying, telling their rosaries, and intoning interminable prayers to the Virgin, in a scandalous competition with the monkeys of the jungle!"[15]

Grandfather was a friend of Martin Demaret, something of a wanderer, who had lived in various parts of Brazil. He had moved from Santarém to a comfortable plantation near Ameri-cana, and through him, Grandfather was able to keep tabs on the Amazon group. He admired the success of R. J. Rhome, who had built up a large plantation, the finest on the Amazon. Rhome had forty slaves, of which four were house servants. The slaves operated a sugar mill and a tobacco-curing establish-ment.

In the 1920s the large Riker family estate, constructed on a tributary of the mighty Amazon River, was dominated by its waterfront manor house, built in the style of antebellum homes in the lower Mississippi Valley. Unlike its neighbors, the house was made of wood. Lush gardens and orchards and colorful tropical trees framed the structure. The massive leaves on the trees wore a variety of browns, yellows and greens. A parrot sat on its perch.

As it turned out, the Confederados in Amazonia had not seen the last of the Yankees. In 1928 the peaceful scene was ruffled by the arrival of a large contingent of Americans, an advance party representing the Ford Motor Car Company of Detroit, then still very much in the grip of its founder, Henry Ford, a man of limitless commercial vision. He, like the Confederate migrants of 1867, considered the Amazon area an untapped treasure, needing only the application of North America know-how and sufficient working capital to bring forth riches—in Ford's case, riches in the form of rubber.

Ford's fame and largess, were far-reaching, and his production methods were successful in the United States, but in Brazil the auto magnate was to suffer failure. Beginning in 1928, Ford had decided to set up a large rubber plantation in an attempt to capture the world market from the Dutch in Java and the British in Ceylon. Ford chose the area fifty miles upstream of the Confederate colony and the frontier town of Santarém, at Boa Vista bluffs. The Brazilian government cooperated and gave him options over several hundred square miles of land, an area only slightly smaller than Connecticut.

After the advance party had left, the citizens of the area awaited, with anticipation, the arrival of the *Norte Americanos* who would transform Amazonia into the rubber capital of the world. As the Rikers, Rhomes, Jenningses, Vaughans, Heningtons, and their children watched from the shores of the Amazon, expecting to be called upon to supply the timber, the foodstuffs, and supplies needed to set up the grand scheme, they saw the loaded ships pass them by and turn up the Tapajós tributary to the landing site. Cleverly, the Yankees from Detroit, following their time-saving habit of making their products on the assembly line, had decided to build everything back home and ship it directly to the plantation and its adjoining industrial complex.

As the natives watched and the wild animals of the rain forest fled in terror, the paternalistic Ford placed an entire American city smack on top of the jungle. All was brought from Detroit—canned and refrigerated food, hospitals, restaurants, shops, bulldozers, sawmills, tennis courts, plumbing, houses (constructed in the American fashion). Everything was destined for this uncivilized country full of monkeys, jaguars, man-eating fish, and snakes. The plan was to require the native workers to live "the American way," in a tightly knit company town, administered by a handfull of supervisors from Detroit, trained in the latest time-and-motion techniques.

U.S. newspapers hailed it as "The Miracle City of the Amazon." Not only was the American value system and culture delivered to Brazil, but a tangible chunk of its concrete and steel resources were transferred as well. It was the Confederados' and their children's first view of post–Civil War America, albeit transplanted.

They were not left out of the operation. Some of the Confederados leased their lands to Ford at profitable rates, and others were recruited into a variety of white-collar jobs. Over three thousand Brazilians were employed to gather the rubber, plant the trees, and run the machinery to process the product. Riker, still vigorous at age seventy-five, worked as an interpreter and even supervised some of the operations. His three sons, too, were given jobs that they kept when they followed the Ford Company back to Detroit.

Unhappily, the endeavor was run by remote control directly from Detroit, where everything was done according to American standards. Henry Ford made all the big decisions and ultimately was responsible for the debacle that occurred. Ex-Confederate Riker, years later, couldn't help laughing when he described the costly venture and how Ford had "attempted, from Michigan, to govern eating habits and table manners among Indios and tropical tramps who flocked to the fabulously generous pay roll and like Oliver Twist, always wanted more . . . nine milreis a day. Tried to give those people patent breakfast food and tinned milk. Fed them at sit-down tables, with waiters and napkins."[16] Uncle Sim's comment from his São Paulo base far to the south was, "They tried to do to these Brazilians what northerners had always wanted to do to the South—Yankeefy it!—and it didn't work there either." Vianna Moog, too, described the scene:

> Suddenly, in the midst of this idyll, the first unexpected trouble. The caboclos, those meek, humble half-breeds, turn into wild beasts. They start by smashing up the whole cafeteria,

they tear everything down. A riot. The officials of the Ford Motor Company run with their families, all terrified, for the freighters anchored in the port. The caboclos, armed with clubs like the French in the taking of the Bastille, march on the strongholds of the directorate and management, roaring something unintelligible to the listeners aboard ship. What can they be shouting about so angrily? Can it be "Down with Mr. Ford!"? Can it be "Down with the Ford Motor Company!"? Nothing of the sort. It appeared that it was a personal disagreement with Popeye the Sailor. What the half-breeds were yelling was, "Down with spinach! No more spinach!" . . . the caboclos were full of boiled spinach and well-vitaminized foods; they could not even look at spinach any more. As for the corn flakes, better not even mention them. . . . enough is enough.

And in one night the officials of the Ford Motor Company learned more sociology than in years at a university. . . . They learned that the caboclos detested the tiled houses in which they lived and the Puritan way of life the officials wished to impose upon them. . . . the houses were veritable ovens, as is easily imaginable when one considers how hot the majority of American houses are in summer. . . . Mr. Ford understood assembly lines and the designs of Divine Providence. He did not, absolutely could not, understand the psychology of the caboclo.[17]

Faced with such serious labor problems and also with technical difficulties in raising the rubber plants in the overly hot Amazonian sun, Ford abandoned the project in the middle 1940s. The Confederados, who had learned how to come to terms with the Amazon and its people and who invested, not millions of dollars, but their own hearts and minds in the area, are still there, Brazilianized.

RACIAL ATTITUDES AS A CROSS-CULTURAL PROBLEM

Ford's approach to Brazil was paternalistic racism. His theory was that he could gain riches by helping the "little brown brothers" in Brazil become Americanized. Together they would then extract the riches of the Amazon and ship them to the industrial colossus in North America.

In his book, Moog analyzed the troubles of the Ford Motor Company alongside the difficulties that occurred in the Confederate migration to Brazil. He, like some observers (there have been precious few), wondered why the Confederates, being American, did not dominate the society around them in the Amazon area, considering their advantage in education and experience. Moog offers the suggestion that, had the migrants to the Amazon been not Confederates but Yankees, they would have overridden the local culture, and the Amazon would be bent to their will. It is an interesting hypothesis but hard to substantiate, as Moog readily admits.

The Ford Motor Company, of course, was not a colonizer, but an amorphous, impersonal, long-range investor and organizer. The company could have learned much from the experience of the Confederado colonists, but the proud automakers arrived wearing ethnocentric blinders. American know-how would triumph over any "underdeveloped" society.

Although the Confederates successfully settled the Amazon, teaching their neighbors new agricultural methods that raised production, they did not add much or change the region around them. José Artur Rios saw racial attitudes as the underlying reason for their lack of impact.

> They imagined they would find in Brazil, a slave-holding country, the same segregation between whites and blacks. The fact is that even in that day, within the Second Empire's society of landed estates and slaves, factors were at work which were to contribute to the peaceful solution of slavery and to the nonexistence of segregation in Brazil. For a long time, for example, the social rise of Negroes and mulattoes had been going on, and the Southerners found themselves, to their stupefaction, in a society in which the color criterion was not the dominant one for social classification. With consternation they saw mulattoes and negroes in the bosom of society, occupying important positions, and, through that fact, ceasing to be regarded as Negroes.[18]

Ballard S. Dunn had tried to acquaint the emigrants with the closeness of black-white relations in Brazil. He mocked the southern emigrant who returned to the U.S. because he couldn't put up with the "negro equality." This Confederate villain of Dunn's story gives up the ghost at the "rude shock of free-negroism, when he espies, at the corner of the street, a man, apparently white, conversing upon terms of perfect equality, with another citizen of the same extraction, as black as can be."[19] Dunn's dissertation on cross-cultural relations scolded Americans at length on the folly of not understanding other nations. He pointed out, for example, that few Americans were aware that Brazilians were descended, not from the Spanish, but from a markedly different people, the Portuguese. "So far from being Spaniards," he wrote, "the Brazilians despise them. . . . they have just pride in their Portuguese language, their mother tongue, which is the elder daughter of the Latin, and boasts a literature second only to that of the French."[20] Were he still alive, Dunn would have been concerned by an article in one of modern-day America's leading magazines stating that the Confederados spoke "Brazilian." Do Canadians speak Canadian?

It is easy in the late twentieth century to feel superior in our racial views to the tired, embittered southern nomads of our story, fresh off creaky little sailing ships in Brazilian ports, who held strong beliefs in their convictions and the superiority of their way of life. They, like most Americans—North or South—had been bonded together as a society by many factors, not the least being the sharply defined black-white racial separation of their daily existence. The cumulative, culture-building processes in the North and South had done their work even by the nineteenth century, and Americans had universally allotted the lowest rung of their social scale to blacks.

Stepping off the gangplank in Brazil, the Confederates were startled as they looked out on this country populated by darker-skinned people. They were clearly uncomfortable, even though they had been warned by their advance scouts and the books published about Brazil.

In matters of social intercourse they received their first lessons in Brazilian living right at dockside. These dark people around them did not lower their eyes in their presence; instead, they looked at them directly. They smiled in a different way and more often. It was impossible much of the time to tell who was boss among the workers. Skin color was not the determining factor, it seemed.

Some of the first-generation Confederados never recovered from the shock of seeing persons of varying colors mixing in a relaxed fashion. They never accustomed themselves to the camaraderie among them or to their custom of kissing and embracing when meeting. A few Confederados struggled to accept the new society they had chosen to escape to, but most older members of the colony never lost the uneasy feeling that they felt in the pit of their stomachs when in the presence, at a social gathering, of persons of notably darker skin.

But all is not what it appears in analyzing the races in Brazil. Skin color, a kind of visual shorthand, has long been the favorite way for humans to pigeonhole themselves, and those in power always play the game to their advantage. But in Brazil the fabric of life had a polka-dot pattern and it was not possible to choose the dark- or light-shaded areas to live in. Those who live in Brazil learn to put the matter in perspective and, not unpredictably, to give it an extremely low priority—at about the level of childish games.

The ironies are irresistible. In Brazil a person is frequently considered white if he had *any* white ancestors. By Brazilian definition, most U.S. blacks are white. Malcolm X, Joe Louis, Barbara Jordan, Martin Luther King, Jesse Jackson, and Lena Horne would have been considered white had they lived in Brazil.

In 1972 I had the opportunity of spending two days with the members of a popular black American dance band. The group was giving a concert at São Paulo's Opera House. They were all black Americans with the exception of a saxophonist, whose ancestors were Portuguese. These black musicians were in confusion during their short visit. When they first arrived, I, as U.S. embassy representative, greeted them at the airport and was given the standard U.S. "white-black, not-too-close, please," treatment. As we proceeded through the city of São Paulo you could see the quizzical looks on the faces of the musicians as they met Brazilians on all sides. For a while they struggled to understand, but by the second night they had retreated within themselves, huddled together, disoriented by their puzzling surroundings where whites and blacks obviously lived as equals. Only the saxophonist was able to mix with those around him, even though he could not understand the Portuguese language spoken by his grandparents.

The immigrant Confederados, similarly, tried to comprehend, struggled to cope, and in the end relied on the values and perceptions imposed on them by their parents and their old society.

When an American anthropologist confronts the problem of defining Brazilian race relations, he is frequently frustrated. Most find their research papers so stuffed with exceptions to whatever rule they have proposed that they are tempted to give up. *Nega*, for example, is used as a term of endearment. *Minha Nega*, literally, "my black girl friend," might be better translated as "my darling." In Brazil men of all ethnic backgrounds apply it with romantic intent to their sweethearts, whether they are black, Japanese, Swedish, Czechoslovakian, or anything else. One of dozens of researchers on the subject, Nelson de Senna wrote: "The problem of racial assimilation and absorption among whites and blacks is a solved problem in Brazil."[21] A Brazilian once asked me, "What's a race riot?" Joaquim Nabuco, the great abolitionist of Brazil, wrote in 1888: "In the United States, during slavery and after, a sharp and rigid line was drawn between the races with relatively little mixing. . . . In Brazil, exactly the opposite took place. Slavery founded on the differences between the races never developed the color line, and in this Brazil was infinitely wiser."[22]

As is their right, some American sociologists have begun recently to criticize the "perfect" race relations in Brazil. They point to the inequalities that occur in Brazilian life, the minimum number of blacks in the Brazilian diplomatic corps, in the navy, and in other fields of endeavor. But the "negroe equality" that confronted the Confederados when their sailing ships arrived in Brazilian ports was not a simple matter of words meant for the pristine, social science laboratory. So jarringly humane were relations among the blacks, mulattoes and whites in Brazil, in contrast to their own "problem" in the United States, that even the most insensitive among them could see the difference. Setting up the straw man of "perfection," makes Brazilian race relations a better target, but it tends to obscure the truth about the story of people who have learned how to work together and to respect each other.

Second- and third-generation Confederados had become somewhat Brazilianized. They, for instance, had a grasp of the racial nuances of Brazilian society. A cultivated person in Brazil was never black. If he owned a nice big fazenda (they had stopped using the term *plantation* by then), he was white for sure. In Brazilian eyes, white and black are used to describe, not a person's race, but his social status. Anyone who is successful, cultivated, or well-to-do is white.

To the absolute horror of the first-generation Confederados (many of whom had fought furiously at Manassas, Gettysburg, and Chickamauga for states' rights, including the right to own black slaves), some of their children began marrying Brazilians, some of whom obviously had Negro blood. They imposed a strong taboo on marriages with Brazilians, insisting that their children marry Americans, preferably from within the Confederado community. A dilemma of sorts was introduced in 1920 when a daughter of one of the most prominent Confederado families, true to the Confederado code, married an American, a black American, who had his own sugarcane plantation in the Santa Barbara area. The act of this young lady seemed to throw a short circuit into the complex cultural bias of the American colonists. There was no outcry— none. The man, after all, was an American, and the couple was welcomed warmly into the colony, now dominated by second- and third-generation Confederados. The Americans, like their Brazilian neighbors, had learned how to change a person from black to white.

In the 1960s, a writer for a U.S. black magazine went to Brazil to find out about reports that racial discrimination in that country did not exist. The writer, Era Bell Thompson, discovered the complexities of Brazilian racial attitudes. Thompson dug deep into the assignment and got a pretty good grasp on the Brazilian way of living peaceably among the races. One of the first interviews was with Dr. and Mrs. James Jones at Americana. Dr. Jones is the grandson of Colonel William Norris of Alabama, one of the Confederado pioneers. Mrs. Jones is descended from Texans. Thompson tells that Mrs. Jones, before the couple made their one and only visit to the United States in 1951, "was not *aware of the race problem* in the States, and said she was not *aware of race* in Brazil" (italics mine).[23] The couple was typical of the Confederados of the twentieth century. The teachings of their parents had been supplanted by the facts of life in Brazilian society.

Thompson had unknowingly touched on the "untainted" aspect of the Confederado colonists. Confederados had managed to avoid the bitterness of the Jim Crow years in America. They had not experienced the American "problem." And neither had I until I made my trip to America in 1935.

GREAT GRANDMOTHER RETURNS FOR A VISIT

One returnee to the United States was Great Grandmother Thatcher. In 1889, true to the vow she took on the deck of the *Derby* and much to the shock of her seven grown children, most of them living in the area around Americana, she announced that she was going back to Marshall, Texas, for a visit. Great Grandmother had been widowed for a year, and the children had assumed that she would live out the rest of her life near them in her spacious plantation house, staffed with servants and very comfortable for a lady in her mid-sixties. But she was adamant. "Hurry! It'll be late fall when we arrive, before the cold weather and the chill blue northers. I must see Texas again before I die, it's been so very long."

The wealthiest of her sons, Simeon, who had made a fortune as a cotton, cane, and watermelon grower, agreed to accompany her on the visit. He had been seven years old when he left, but could still remember some of their life in east Texas.

The family received the letter telling of her death one month after her arrival in Marshall. Simeon wrote that the shock of travel and readjusting to the South had been too much for her. "She just couldn't understand how it could have changed so in the thirty years since she had left."

Reverend Ballard S. Dunn, the New Orleans Episcopalian minister who led the largest contingent of colonists to Brazil, appears in this engraving.

Epilogue

THERE is something especially terrifying about having the only route to your home blocked. Father was at his office on the eighteenth floor of the Noite Building and Mother and I were downtown shopping when the alarm and call to arms was sounded. It was civil war. Armies of the rebellious states of Brazil had moved swiftly and were beginning to surround Rio de Janeiro that morning. Rio was especially vulnerable from the sea, and father looked from his office window to see if the attacking naval forces from the state of São Paulo were streaming into Guanabara Bay.

We knew that the first act of the army would be to block the tunnel leading to our home in Ipanema. The tunnel was our link to mid-Rio (O Centro). Through it father went to work every morning. Through it, accompanied by a maid, I rode the open-air electric trolley to Bennett School. There was no gunfire that day, but the sound of the big metal shutters clanging shut on every store was enough. The shutters were always pulled down noisily in times of trouble, and the Cariocas, residents of Rio, were attuned to the sound. It was not until evening that the word went out that Paulistas were not at the gates of Rio but were in fact being pummeled by the federal forces a hundred miles south on the rail line to São Paulo. Only then was the traffic tunnel through the mountain opened, and we could go home.

The rebellion began on July 9, 1932, led by the state of São Paulo, by far the richest in Brazil. This state had become

121

the "Heart of Brazil." Its plantations were the largest and most productive, and it possessed considerable industrial resources. In the beginning it had the support of several other states, but quick action by the federal forces and the maneuverings of dictator Getulio Vargas had isolated the Paulistas. It was 6.5 million against the rest of Brazil, a nation of 35 million people. My mother's heart was with the Paulistas, though she had been living in Rio for seventeen years. Both of her brothers, Yancey and Gibson, and many of our Confederado cousins were fighting with the "states' rights" armies of São Paulo against the federal government of Brazil. But she knew that theirs was a hopeless cause.

The Confederados in the state, though few compared to immigrant Italians and Germans, gave added interest to the accounts of the conflict published in the United States. One writer, Lawrence Hill, reported that he had received from one of the Confederados, Martha Norris of São Paulo, an anxious letter "which reveals much solicitation for several of the woman's grandsons who are now fighting in the rebel army and who feel certain of victory over the government. . . . hundreds of others with Southern lineage are playing roles in Brazilian history."[1] The war apparently was big news in the United States. The *New York Times* and other American newspapers headlined it. They even sent several correspondents down to cover the story. In one *New York Times* account, the reporter used the American Reconstruction term *carpetbaggers* in describing the federals in São Paulo.[2]

Confederados in São Paulo had rushed to support their state. Centro Academico Horace Lane's faculty and student body declared themselves on the side of the rebels. Students from MacKenzie University took to the streets, shouting their support of the secessionist cause. Many of them enlisted in the Paulista army. Some were drafted or were brought into the engagement because they were members of the state guard. We began to receive word that some of our friends and cousins had died in the fierce battle raging to the west of Rio de Janeiro. We knew that São Paulo, standing alone, with its seaports blockaded, could not hold out for long.

The delights of living on the beautiful beach in Rio de

Janeiro were destroyed when the war began. The federal military appeared all around us, and there was terror in the eyes of our neighbors. Bayonets, machine guns, hand grenades, and other mad instruments of war suddenly became very real, close enough to touch.

One day I was bouncing a soccer ball on the hot sidewalk in front of my house, avoiding the puddles of water left by the street washers, who had just passed in their tank truck. I saw a car turn onto our street from Ipanema Avenue and drive slowly along, not far from the curb. As it arrived almost exactly in front of my house, the car door swung open, and two men jumped out and grabbed a well-dressed man who was walking not ten feet away from me. They dragged him into the vehicle, and the driver pulled quickly away. I saw that they were hitting him with their fists as he lay across the back seat. He didn't cry out, though there was fear on his face.

I ran and told Mother, who calmed me down. I could see that she was very worried, however. We were Brazilian Paulistas, living in the federal capital, much like some of the southerners who were living in Washington, DC, at the start of the Civil War, afraid of being accused of espionage, disloyalty, even treason. Mother said it was probably the police, taking somebody in for interrogation, but the incident heightened the tension at our house.

The two armies fought fiercely for control of the railroad lines between the cities of Rio and São Paulo. The federals captured many prisoners, incarcerating them on Rija Island north of the capital city. Mother saw some of them marched from the downtown railway station and wondered if her brothers were among them.

More ominous to us in Rio was the news that the federals had bombed Campinas, the city nearest to Americana, where many Confederados now lived. The Rio newspaper *O'Noite* said there were many casualties, including women and children, but details were sketchy. Americana itself was on the main route of the attacking federal army.

One of the newspapers mentioned that former president Calvin Coolidge had compared the events in Brazil to the American Civil War. *Outlook* magazine reported: "Certainly the large-scale military operations in Brazil resemble the Virginia campaigns of the 1860s more than they do the street fighting which has overturned other South American governments this year. This is not just another one of the perennial banana uprisings of the tropics."[3] The press reported that more than 130,000 troops were engaged, supported by modern artillery and airplanes.

Suddenly, on October 3 we heard the announcement of a peace settlement. General Bert Klinger, the chief of staff of the Paulista forces, signed the agreement. His ammunition was low, several railway lines having been cut, and Campinas was threatened with capture as federal forces overwhelmed the rebel army. Vargas, in a radio address, announced the terms of surrender. Apparently magnanimous in victory, he allowed the rebels to keep their weapons, but he demanded the arrest and deportation of all their leaders.

Several days after the announcement, we heard a knock at our side door. We opened it and there stood Uncle Yancey Harris, mother's brother, with his wife and twelve-year-old daughter. They came in quickly. As an officer in the rebellious São Paulo State Guard he was among those liable for imprisonment or deportation, and he told us that he wanted to be hidden until things calmed down. Without hesitation we took them in and gave them rooms on the second floor of our big stucco house. There they stayed, seldom straying outdoors, for three months until the dictator, seeking to reduce the bitterness left by the war, offered total amnesty to all the rebels.

Vargas, a shrewd political leader, calmed the atmosphere by declaring that the federal government would pay all the rebel states' war debts, even honoring their hastily printed currency and war bonds. A few of the Confederados wondered what the United States would be like in modern times had the Yankees done the same. Despite Vargas's efforts at patching up the wounds of the struggle, the Paulistas remember. One can still see an occasional gold lapel pin in São Paulo with "32" engraved on it, the year of the big war. The buttons are reminiscent of the "Forget—Hell!" emblems one still sees occasionally in the American South. Ironically, about three years after the civil war in Brazil, my father decided that he would return to the United States, and on July 12, 1935, we sailed from Rio de Janeiro.

AMERICAN DESCENDANTS' FRATERNITY

It wasn't until December 4, 1955, that the Confederate descendants got around to organizing themselves formally. As the size of the groups that used to gather at the Confederate Cemetery became smaller and smaller there was a feeling among these twentieth-century Confederates that their experience was unique and worth remembering. They became the Fraternidade Descendencia Americana (American Descendants' Fraternity), "descendants of the old United States [Confederate] colony, linked by ties of friendship, without reference to religious or political creed united in solid fraternal bond." (The logo of the organization is a triangle showing two hands meeting in a handclasp, surrounded by the name.)

It was none too soon. Most of the descendants had long since migrated to the big cities, just like their distant cousins back in North America. The cemetery with its monument, small church, and neat grounds is the sentimental heart of the Confederado settlement in that huge country. Unfortunately, as the new generations are born far away in other parts of Brazil, the level of support seems to decrease and the church, museum, and grounds have suffered neglect. Periodically the organization has required an infusion of funds to keep it going.

It looks as if a new chapel will soon have to be built, the third. The present one was constructed in 1933 and is showing signs of decay. Both Protestants and Catholics contributed funds to its construction. The museum area needs help. Some of the exhibits (wagons, plows, and a sewing machine brought from the Confederacy) are deteriorating.

The members and their guests meet four times a year at an all-day picnic, with a covered-dish lunch and loosely scheduled special events. The meeting is usually on a Sunday, and begins with a service in the little chapel where the altar is covered with the three flags, Brazilian, Confederate, and U.S.

Appendix: Family Names

Some of the family names of the migrants to Brazil are listed below:

Andersen	Buchanan	Cole
Armstrong	Budd	Colter
Ashee	Buford	Cook
Ayers	Buhlow	Combs
Bagby	Bulfatin	Cottingham
Baird	Bunnel	Coulter
Bankston	Burns	Cowley
Barnsley	Burrand	Crawley
Barr	Burton	Crovey
Baujahn	Byington	Crisp
Beasley	Campbell	Cullen
Bentley	Capps	Currie
Berney	Carlton	Daguerre
Blackford	Carr	Daniel
Bloxom	Carrington	Dascomb
Blue	Carlton	Darvile
Boeringer	Carson	Davis
Bookwalter	Carter	Demaret
Bowen	Cencir	DeYambert
Boyd	Censon	Dickie
Braxton	Chaffie	Dickson
Britt	Chamberlain	Dillard
Broadnax	Cherry	Dire
Brooks	Clark	Dobbins
Brown	Clayburn	Dodson
Brownlow	Coachman	Doherty
Bruce	Cobb	Domm
Bryant	Cogburn	Dowds

Dozier	Hardis	Linden
Drain	Hargrove	Linn
Dresback	Harris	Lloyd
Dumas	Harrison	McAlpine
Dunn	Harvey	McCann
Dyer	Hastings	McDade
Easton	Hawthorne	McDonald
Ellis	Heinsman	McEachin
Emmett	Henderson	McFadden
Emerson	Henington	McIntyre
Ezelle	Hickman	McGee
Falwood	Hogan	McKnight
Fahay	Holland	McMullan
Farley	Howard	McNabb
Feagin	Howell	Malone
Fenley	Howes	Marchant
Ferguson	Hunter	Mason
Fielder	Isaacs	Massey
Fife	Jackson	Mastiff
Fletcher	James	Maston
Frelder	Jennings	Mathews
Foster	Johnson	Maxwell
Fox	Joiner	Mendenhall
Freleigh	Jones	Meriwether
Gammon	Judkins	Miller
Gannon	Keese	Mills
Garlington	Keeps	Minchin
Garner	Keith	Moncrief
Gaston	Kemper	Moore
Gates	Kennedy	Morgan
German	Kennerly	Morrison
Gill	Kernan	Morton
Gilmore	Kerr	Murphy
Guillet	Keyes	Myers
Glenn	King	Nathan
Godfrey	Kirk	Nelius
Gottschalk	Knuse	Nettles
Grady	Koger	Newman
Graham	Kolb	Nichols
Green	Kollinger	Nollens
Gunter	Kramer	Norris
Hall	Landers	Northrup
Hanny	Lane	Odell
Hanson	Lang	Oliver
Hardeman	Le Conte	Owen

Paine	Rowe	Tovamjer
Parcher	Russell	Townsend
Parker	Sampson	Trigg
Parks	Sanders	Turner
Patterson	Schofield	Vaughn
Peacock	Scurlock	Velaky
Penn	Seawright	Vincent
Perkins	Sexton	Waddell
Peter	Seymour	Wade
Peterson	Shares	Wallace
Pettigrew	Sharpley	Ward
Philips	Shaw	Warne
Pichowski	Shippey	Warson
Pierce	Slaughter	Watson
Pinkney	Smith	Watts
Pitts	Sparks	Weaver
Platt	Spencer	Webster
Porter	Stamply	Weingeutter
Prestridge	Steagall	Weissinger
Proston	Steele	Wells
Provost	Stewart	Wesson
Pyles	Stiel	Wharton
Quillen	Stone	Whitman
Quilly	Stow	Whitaker
Radcliff	Strong	White
Rader	Stuk	Whitehead
Raidig	Swain	Wright
Rainey	Tanner	Williamson
Ralston	Tarver	Wingeter
Ransom	Taylor	Wise
Rast	Terrell	Wiggins
Rean	Thatcher	Wood
Rhome	Thomas	Wright
Riker	Thompson	Yancey
Ritter	Tilly	Young
Roussel	Tobin	

Notes

Chapter 1. THE ETERNAL REMEMBRANCE

1. Paul I. Wellman, *The House Divides* (Garden City, N.Y.: Doubleday, 1966), 184–85.
2. Ibid.
3. Shelby Foote, *The Civil War* (New York: Random House, 1963), 926.
4. Ibid., 936–37.
5. Horace Porter, *Campaigning with Grant* (New York: Crown, 1957), 511.
6. C. H. Wesley, *Collapse of the Confederacy* (Washington, D.C.: Associated Publishers, 1937), 93.
7. Hodding Carter, *The Angry Scar* (Garden City, N.Y.: Doubleday, 1959), 33.

Chapter 2. NIGHT IS THE BEGINNING AND THE END

1. T. Lynn Smith, *Brazil: People and Institutions* (Baton Rouge: Louisiana State University Press, 1967), 162.
2. Blanche Henry Clark Weaver, "Confederate Immigrants in Brazil," *Journal of Southern History*, 18 (Feb., 1952), 446–48.
3. Vianna Moog, *Bandeirantes and Pioneers* (New York: George Braziller, 1964), 37.
4. *Montgomery Advertiser*, August 10, 1867.
5. Frank Shippey to Ballard Dunn, June 2, 1866, Ballard S. Dunn, *Brazil: the Home for Southerners* (New York: Richardson, 1866), 71.
6. George Washington Keyes to General A. T. Hawthorne, Aug. 1869, in Julia L. Keyes, *Our Life in Brazil* (Nyack, New York: N. H. Huber, 1967), 256.
7. Andrew F. Rolle, *The Lost Cause* (Norman: University of Oklahoma Press, 1965), 45.
8. General Wade Hampton to Jefferson Davis, in Sam Carter, *The Last Cavaliers* (New York: St. Martin, 1974), 315–16.
9. Rolle, *The Lost Cause*, 45.
10. Ibid., 31.

11. Robert E. Lee, *Recollections and Letters of General Robert E. Lee* (New York: Garden City, 1926), 163.

12. Ibid., 165.

13. Ibid., 162.

14. Ibid., 164.

15. Jefferson Davis, *Rise and Fall of the Confederate Government* (New York: Thomas Yoseloff, 1958), 699.

16. Dunn, *Brazil: The Home for Southerners*, 24–25.

17. Lawrence Durrell, *Limões Amargos, 1970* (London: Faber and Faber, 1970), 3.

18. Stephen Birnbaum, *South America, 1983* (Boston: Houghton Mifflin, 1983), 478.

19. Lansford W. Hastings, *The Emigrant's Guide to Brazil* (New York: Hastings, 1865), 20–21.

20. *Columbus (Ga.) Enquirer*, November 5, 1865.

21. Matthew Fontaine Maury, *The Amazon and the Atlantic Slopes of South America* (Washington, D.C.: Maury, 1853), 40.

22. *Mobile Daily Register*, Nov. 17, 1869.

23. *Nashville Union & Dispatch*, July 1, 1868.

24. Thomas Griffin, "Confederate Colonies Along the Amazon River" *Brazil Herald*, March 28, 1981.

25. Smith, *Brazil*, 423.

26. James E. Edmonds, "They've Gone Back Home!" *Saturday Evening Post*, Jan. 4, 1941, pp. 30–47.

27. Moog, *Bandeirantes and Pioneers*, 41.

28. Edmonds, "They've Gone-Back Home!" 30–47.

Chapter 3. Noah's Ark

1. Lawrence F. Hill, *Diplomatic Relations with Latin America* (Austin: University of Texas Press, 1936), 20.

2. Blanche Henry Clark Weaver, "Confederate Emigration to Brazil," *Journal of Southern History*, 27 (Feb., 1961), 37–38.

3. Ibid., 38.

4. Col. James McFadden Gaston, *Hunting a Home in Brazil* (Philadelphia: King and Baird, 1867), 291–92.

5. Ibid., 42.

6. Weaver, "Confederate Emigration to Brazil," 38.

7. Julia L. Keyes, *Our Life in Brazil* (Nyack, N.Y.: N. H. Huber, 1967), 12.

8. Ibid., 24–25.

9. Ballard S. Dunn, *Brazil: The Home for Southerners* (New York: Richardson, 1866), 37.

10. Ibid., 55–77.

11. Eliza Kerr Shippey, "When Americans Were Immigrants," *Kansas City Journal*, June 16, 1912, p. 4.

12. Keyes, *Our Life in Brazil*, 7.

13. Ibid., 9–11.

14. Shippey, "When Americans Were Immigrants," 4.

15. Keyes, *Our Life in Brazil*, 21–22.

16. *New Orleans Times*, Dec. 1, 1867.

17. Ibid.

18. Edwin McDowell," Confederate Outpost in Brazil," *Wall Street Journal*, Aug. 22, 1975, p. 11.

19. Keyes, *Our Life in Brazil*, 44.

20. Frank P. Goldman, *Os Pioneiros Americanos no Brasil* (Philadelphia: King and Baird, 1972), 12.

21. Keyes, *Our Life in Brazil*, 37.

22. Weaver, "Confederate Emigration to Brazil," 40–41.

23. Goldman, *Os Pioneiros Americanos*, 31.

24. Eugene C. Harter, *Lithopinion Magazine*, No. 39, Sept. 1975, p. 41.

25. Judith McKnight Jones, *Soldado Descansa!* (São Paulo: Jar De, 1967), 143.

26. Hill, *Confederate Exodus to Latin America*, 39–40.

27. Charles Wagley, *Brazil* (New York: Columbia University Press, 1979), 160–80.

28. *Atlanta Journal*, Oct. 8, 1965.

Chapter 4. AMERICAN CITY, BRAZIL

1. Frances Cawthon, "Look Away, Look Away!" *Atlanta Journal and Constitution*, Feb. 3, 1974, p. 23.

2. Vianna Moog, *Bandeirantes and Pioneers* (New York: Braziller, 1964), 40.

3. Gilberto Freyre, *New World in the Tropics* (New York: Knopf 1959) 136.

4. Ibid., 194.

5. Mark Jefferson, "An American Colony in Brazil," *Geographical Review*, April 1928, p. 231.

6. Hodding Carter, *The Angry Scar* (Garden City, New York: Doubleday 1959), 393.

7. Ibid., 222–29.

Chapter 5. A CONFEDERADO MISCELLANY

1. Gilberto Freyre, *New World in the Tropics* (New York: Knopf, 1959), 194.

2. Blanche Henry Clark Weaver, "Confederate Immigrants in Brazil," *Journal of Southern History*, 18 (Feb., 1951), 447.

3. Ibid., 449.

4. Judith McKnight Jones, *Soldado Descansa!* (São Paulo: Jar De, 1967), 222.

5. Philip Jessup, *The Biography of Elihu Root* (New York: Dodd, Meade, 1938), 483–84.

6. Letter to *Columbus* (Ga.) *Sun Times* from Hervey Hall, Feb. 5, 1867.

7. Ibid.

8. Jones, *Soldado Descansa!*, 246.

9. Weaver, "Confederate Immigrants in Brazil," 459.

10. Louis Bromfield, *From My Experience* (New York: Harper, 1955), 100.

11. Ibid., 100–102.

12. Ibid., 101–102n.

13. Frank P. Goldman, *Os Pioneiros Americanos no Brasil* (Philadelphia: King and Baird, 1972), 10.

14. Thomas Griffin, "Confederate Colonies Along the Amazon River," *Brazil Herald*, March 28, 1981.

15. Euclides da Cunha, *A Margem da Historia* (Rio: Lello & Irmão, 1946), 108–09.

16. James E. Edmonds, "They've Gone-Back Home!" *Saturday Evening Post*, Jan. 4, 1941, p. 47.

17. Vianna Moog, *Bandeirantes and Pioneers* (New York: George Braziller, 1964), 29–30.

18. José Artur Rios, "A Imigração de Confederados Norte-Americanos no Brasil," *Revista de Imigração e Colonização* (Dec.–Jan., 1949), 17.

19. Ballard S. Dunn, *Brazil: The Home for Southerners* (New York: Richardson, 1866), 19.

20. Ibid., 42–43.

21. Nelson de Senna, *Africanos no Brasil* (Brasil: Belo Horizonte, 1938), 48.

22. Joaquim Nabuco, *O Abolicionismo* (São Paulo: São Paulo, 1944), 149–51.

23. Era Bell Thompson, "Amalgamation," *Ebony Magazine* (Sept. 1965), 36.

Epilogue

1. Lawrence F. Hill, *Diplomatic Relations with Latin America* (Austin: University of Texas Press, 1936), 75.

2. "Fierce Fight Rages on São Paulo Front," *New York Times*, Aug. 20, 1932, p. 8.

3. "Background in Brazil," *Outlook Magazine*, Oct. 22, 1930, p. 288.

Index